MAJOR EVENTS IN

WORLD HISTORY

50 DEFINING MOMENTS from ANCIENT CIVILIZATIONS to the MODERN DAY

A World History Book for Kids

Susan B. Katz, NBCT

Illustrations by
Meel Tamphanon

ROCKRIDGE PRESS

For Darryl and Crystal, who took the time to help me better understand and appreciate many of the topics in this book, and for Michelle, Jim, and Chalmers, who gave invaluable input.

Series Designer: Brian Lewis
Interior and Cover Designer: Scott Petrower
Art Producer: Janice Ackerman
Editor: Mary Colgan
Production Editor: Jenna Dutton
Production Manager: Michael Kay

Illustration © 2021 Meel Tamphanon. Author photo courtesy of Jeanne Marquis Photography.

Hardcover ISBN: 978-1-63878-599-6 | Paperback ISBN: 978-1-64876-370-0
eBook ISBN: 978-1-64876-371-7
R0

CONTENTS

Ocean

THE HISTORY OF THE WORLD

*Full knowledge of the past helps
us in dealing with the future.*

—Theodore Roosevelt

The people, places, and problems of the past might seem unimportant, but nothing could be further from the truth. Learning how technology was invented, why wars were fought, or how countries were formed helps us understand our world today so we can avoid repeating dangerous mistakes. From ancient civilizations to modern times, this book grounds us in 50 major events that shaped the world.

A Brief Journey Through Time

We have divided these world historical events into seven time periods: Ancient Civilization, the Middle Ages, the Age of Exploration and Reformation, the Age of Revolution and Enlightenment, the Age of Imperialism and Industry, World Wars and the Rise of the Modern Era, and Post–World War II and Modern Times. The book begins with the oldest known civilization and traces how life changed over time, all the way to the present day. (Note: BCE means Before the Common Era. The years in BCE count down to 1. Now we are in the Common Era [CE] and we count up.)

Ancient Civilization (3999 BCE–300 CE)

The Middle Ages (500–1500 CE)

The Age of Exploration and Reformation (1400s–1600s CE)

The Age of Revolution and Enlightenment (1685–1848 CE)

The Age of Imperialism and Industry (1850–1914 CE)

World Wars and the Rise of the Modern Era (1914–1945 CE)

Post–World War II and Modern Times (1946 CE–present day)

50 Defining Moments

This book lays out 50 defining moments in world history. A "defining moment" is an event that changed the course of history in some significant way. These events were chosen because they paved the way for new inventions, impacted the world in a major way, or formed the foundation of elements that are still in existence today, like religion or newly formed countries. Because this book highlights only 50 events, it can't possibly cover *everything* important in world history, but it aims to give a solid overview of major events, time periods, places, and changes throughout the history of the world.

Covering everything from political leaders to the beginnings of world religions, this book gives you a sense of how all the global pieces fit together. You will find that there were many wars, revolutions, and battles over the course of time. Often, these fights were struggles over land, religion, or resources. Some events are difficult to read about, but important to learn. Slavery, the Holocaust in World War II, and the terrorist attacks against the United States on September 11, 2001, were tragic, but learning about them can prevent people from repeating history. Let's start way back in time and imagine what life was like thousands of years ago.

MESOPOTAMIA

4000–2000 BCE

Six thousand years ago, the area in southwest Asia between the Tigris and Euphrates Rivers was called Mesopotamia, which means "between two rivers." The earliest human civilizations lived here in city-states ruled by kings. City-states were cities that governed themselves and the land around them. Mesopotamia is often called the "cradle of civilization" because important inventions like the wheel, writing, and the plow, and concepts like math, time, and maps began here.

From 4000 to 2000 BCE, a civilization called Sumer controlled Mesopotamia. The Sumerian city-states occupied an area of Mesopotamia that is now part of Iraq and Kuwait. These city-states competed against each other and were the first to create professional armies and large central governments. Mesopotamians also buried treasures in the tombs of their rulers to prepare the leaders for their next life. Sumerians believed in many gods.

In around 3200 BCE, Sumerians also developed the first written language, called "cuneiform," to help people keep records of goods bought and sold. Cuneiform was a series of symbols pressed into clay tablets that were then left in the sunshine to dry. These symbols later led to letters, words, and sentences. People called scribes carved the writing onto these tablets. Sumerians also created the way we tell time, where 60 seconds equals one minute and 60 minutes equals one hour.

Uruk, the first city-state in Mesopotamia, was founded by the Sumerians around 4000 BCE. People traded goods, made large public art sculptures and mosaics, and constructed huge columns and temples. At the height of Uruk, about 50,000 people lived there.

The oldest known piece of literature, or fiction, also came from Mesopotamia. It is an epic poem called the *Epic of Gilgamesh*, which tells the story of a Sumerian king named Gilgamesh who wanted to live forever. It was written in cuneiform on 12 clay tablets. In 1872 CE, the archeologist George Smith translated part of the *Epic of Gilgamesh* into English. Before these tablets were discovered and deciphered, people thought the Bible was the oldest book in the world.

Much of what began in Mesopotamia built a foundation for the way later societies were established and grew. Mesopotamian inventions, from the concept of time to buying and selling goods at market, continue to shape how we live today.

HISTORY REVEALED

Some historians believe that biblical stories like the Fall of Man, the Great Flood, and the Garden of Eden may have started as Mesopotamian myths, although the Great Flood story was recorded in many different religions and regions, and may have been inspired by real events.

EXPLORE MORE!

The Gilgamesh Trilogy by Ludmila Zeman includes stories about Gilgamesh the King and the revenge of Ishtar.

BABYLONIA AND THE CREATION OF HAMMURABI'S CODE

1792–1750 BCE

Hammurabi's Code is one of the earliest known written set of laws. These laws laid out how crimes should be punished in Babylonia.

By the time he died in 1750 BCE, King Hammurabi of Babylon had united most of the Mesopotamian city-states under his control. King Hammurabi made this region, called Babylonia, and its capital of Babylon, into a strong military power. He ruled from 1792 to 1750 BCE. The king constructed many buildings, created a government, traded with India and Egypt, and charged taxes.

Most famously, King Hammurabi created a code of laws, carved it on huge, finger-shaped stone pillars, and put it in public for all to see. The Babylonian empire was based on these 282 laws, known as Hammurabi's Code, which everyone had to follow.

These laws helped Hammurabi rule Babylonia by clearly defining punishments for different crimes. They were based on the rule "an eye for an eye," meaning that a punishment should be equal to the crime. For example, if a man broke another man's arm, the punishment was to break the first man's arm, too. Punishments could change depending on the criminal's class (how rich or poor they were). This code also gave the government a lot of power, and their punishments were often violent. Accused people did not have lawyers to help defend them, unlike in many legal systems today. Eventually, the stone with Hammurabi's Code on it was stolen by invaders and was not rediscovered until 1901!

Hammurabi also built thick walls all around the city of Babylon. The Greeks later wrote that the walls were so wide they could race chariots atop them. The city was about 3.5 square miles (9 square kilometers).

At the main entrance of Babylon, there was a portal called the Ishtar Gate. It was decorated with bricks painted bright blue and images of animals like lions, bulls, and dragons.

The Babylonian empire fell apart after King Hammurabi died and, for centuries, was just a small kingdom. Hammurabi's Code influenced how other cultures made laws. Though legal systems have changed over the centuries, people are still punished for crimes they commit.

HISTORY REVEALED

In the Bible, the Tower of Babel is said to have been made by humans to try to reach heaven. According to the story, when God saw the tower, he destroyed it and spread people around the globe, speaking all different languages, so they could not understand each other.

EXPLORE MORE!

You can visit the Metropolitan Museum of Art (the Met) either in person in New York City or online at MetMuseum.org to learn more about Babylonia.

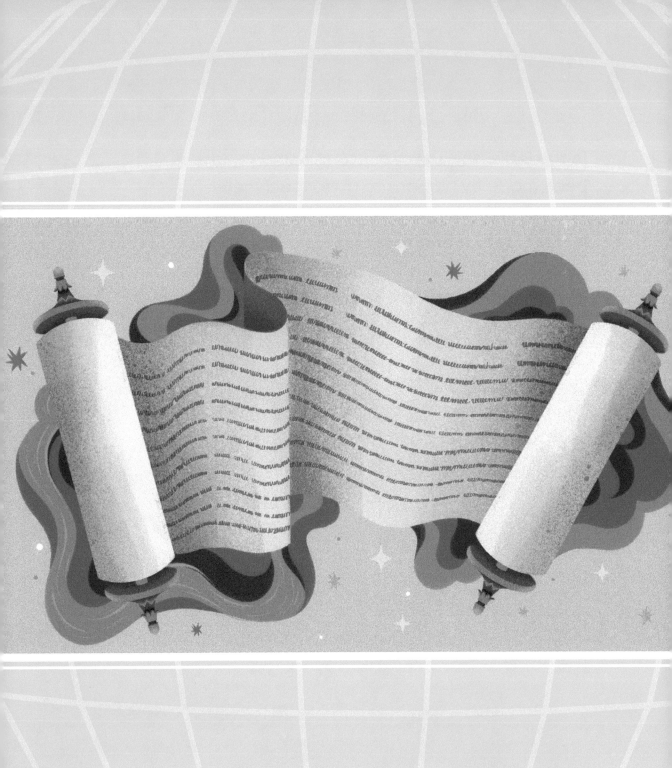

ABRAHAM: THE FATHER OF THREE FAITHS

(596–530s BCE)

Abraham was the "father of three faiths," or religions: Judaism, Christianity, and Islam. These religions are sometimes called the Abrahamic religions.

Judaism began about 4,000 years ago. According to the Bible, the leader of Judaism was a man named Abraham. Abraham was long considered to be the first person who worshipped, or believed in and prayed to, a single god. Abraham and his wife, Sarah, had a son named Isaac. Isaac later had a son named Jacob, who is said to have been the father of the children who created Israel, the Jewish nation-state.

Around 1006–965 BCE, a king named David ruled the city of Jerusalem, where the Israelites (what Jewish people used to be called) lived. Jewish people believe that there were stone tablets in a chest, called the Ark of the Covenant, in Jerusalem on which the Ten Commandments written by God could be found. The Ten Commandments, or sacred laws, state how

Jewish people should live their lives. The commandments tell people to not steal, lie, harm others, be jealous, or disrespect their parents and neighbors. Dozens of countries' laws are based around the Ten Commandments.

Because Christianity came from Judaism, the two religions together are often called Judeo-Christianity. Although there are many differences between the two religions, there are many similarities as well. One important similarity is that Christians also believe the Ten Commandments are rules from God that tell them how to live. Christians and Jewish people also share the belief that people should "love thy neighbor as you love thyself." The Christian Bible traces the ancestry of Jesus back to King David, Isaac, and Abraham. This is why Abraham is known as the father of Christianity, too.

Muslims, who practice the religion of Islam, believe in Abraham as a prophet. In the Quran, the main religious text of Islam, Abraham is described as a messenger of Allah (the Arabic word for God). Muslims call him Ibrahim, and his name is mentioned in their daily prayers many times.

Today, there are approximately 2.5 billion Christians in the world, 1.9 billion Muslims, and 15 million Jewish people. These numbers mean that roughly 57 percent of the people in the world practice an Abrahamic religion.

HISTORY REVEALED

The Egyptian pharaoh Akhenaten created the first known monotheistic religion, called Atenism, based around one god. Later pharaohs tried to erase Atenism from history, but it was rediscovered by 19th- and 20th-century philosophers.

EXPLORE MORE!

You can read the Ten Commandments, which were originally written in Hebrew, here:

- You shall have no other gods but me.
- You shall not make or worship any idols.
- You shall not misuse the name of the Lord your God.
- You shall remember and keep the Sabbath day holy.
- Respect your father and mother.
- You must not murder.
- You must not take someone else's husband or wife.
- You must not steal.
- You must not lie.
- You must not be envious.

BUDDHISM AND SIDDHARTHA GAUTAMA

563–483 BCE

Siddhartha Gautama was an Indian Hindu prince who saw suffering in the world and meditated, or sat quietly breathing, to figure out how to help relieve people's pain. He became known as the Buddha.

Somewhere between 563 and 483 BCE, an Indian Hindu prince named Siddhartha Gautama led a fancy life until he explored beyond his palace in the Himalayan mountains. He saw that many people were suffering, poor, and sick. He decided to leave his life of luxury and figure out the meaning of life in order to help heal humans from suffering. Siddhartha Gautama became the Buddha, or "Enlightened One," which means someone who is awake and aware in every moment to the joys and suffering felt by themselves and others. His teachings became the foundation of Buddhism.

Legend has it that the Buddha sat under a tree, without food, for 49 days. Using knowledge gained from this deep meditation, he taught the Four Noble Truths to millions of people. These truths talk about how someone can end suffering by giving up desire and stopping themselves from wanting material things or trying to change a situation. He took the Four Noble Truths and explained them further for his followers through the Eightfold Path which is a set of guidelines for reaching enlightenment.

The Eightfold Path teaches: 1) Right understanding of the Buddha's teachings; 2) Right intention; 3) Right speech, or not lying or saying anything mean; 4) Right action, or not killing, stealing, or hurting others; 5) Right livelihood, or having a job that brings about happiness, joy, and peace in the world; 6) Right effort, or being a positive person; 7) Right mindfulness, or staying aware of your mind, body, and emotions; and 8) Right concentration, or living in the moment, and focusing on the present, not the past or future, so you can think clearly.

What is known as the "dharma," or Buddha's teachings, is shared in Buddhist temples from the United States to China to South Africa. Now other Buddhist leaders like the Dalai Lama and Thich Nhat Hanh are listened to as well. Buddhism is the fourth most practiced religion today, with more than 500 million people following the Buddha's teachings from almost every country in the world.

HISTORY REVEALED

The Buddha hesitated to teach the dharma to others who might be led by hatred, greed, and ignorance. So he meditated for another 49 days. According to legend, the god Brahma Sahampati convinced him that some people "with little dust in their eyes" would understand, so the Buddha agreed to share his wisdom.

EXPLORE MORE!

Meditation and mindfulness can help people of all ages reduce stress and feel happier. Look for *Mindfulness for Kids in 10 Minutes a Day* by Maura Bradley to find simple ways to bring a mindfulness practice into your daily life.

THE GREEK EMPIRE AND ALEXANDER THE GREAT

700s–146 BCE

Greece is sometimes called the "cradle of modern western civilization." One of its greatest rulers was Alexander III of Macedon, known to history as Alexander the Great.

The Greeks believed in many gods, not just one. Zeus and Hera were the king and queen of all the gods. Dozens of other gods and goddesses were believed to each have power over a particular part of the world. For example, Poseidon was the god of the sea. Aphrodite was the goddess of love. Myths about these gods show us how the Greeks used stories to understand and explain their world. Many Greeks also wrote plays and acted them out in large outdoor theaters.

Around 776 BCE, the Greeks began a sports competition and festival to honor the gods. It was called the Olympics and it took place regularly for 12 centuries. The original Olympics included poetry, running, jumping, discus throwing, wrestling, boxing, martial arts, and chariot races. Even today, the

Olympics are a global sporting event where athletes from hundreds of countries gather to compete.

The Greeks also inspired a form of government used by many countries today. Pericles, a Greek statesman, asked for citizens' opinions on laws and official decisions, establishing the foundation for what we call democracy.

Another important part of Greek life was philosophy, the study of ideas about knowledge, reasoning, and values. Famous Greek philosophers include Socrates, Plato, and Aristotle. One of Aristotle's students was a 13-year-old boy named Alexander.

Alexander III of Macedon was the son of King Philip II. Alexander came to power in Greece when his father was killed in 336 BCE. He was only 20 years old when he took the throne. He was the king from about 336 to 323 BCE. During that time, he transformed Greece into one of the largest and most powerful empires in the ancient world.

Alexander invaded the Persian Empire, Egypt, and some of India. He was a powerful and strategic military leader and spread Greek culture throughout the areas he conquered. His impact was so significant that after his death people called him Alexander the Great. When he died, his empire split into four kingdoms: most of Persia, Egypt and part of Persia, Greece and Macedonia, and Turkey.

Many aspects of the modern world have roots that reach back into ancient Greece. Greek mythology, the Olympics, philosophy, democracy, and ancient theater have all had an influence on the way we live now.

HISTORY REVEALED

Modern-day marathons also came from Greece. In 490 BCE, a soldier ran about 25 miles from the battlefield near Marathon, Greece, to Athens to tell everyone Greece had defeated the Persians. After the soldier delivered the message, he fell over and died! Still, runners continue to train for and compete in marathons, running 26.2 miles (about 42 kilometers) every year.

EXPLORE MORE!

Read *Goddess Power: A Kids' Book of Greek and Roman Mythology: 10 Empowering Tales of Legendary Women* by Yung In Chae for more about Greek mythology.

THE ROMAN EMPIRE AND FALL OF THE GREEK EMPIRE

(Fall of the Greek Empire: 146 BCE;
Roman Empire: 31 BCE–1453 CE)

Not far from Greece, in Rome, Italy, another empire had been growing. The Roman Empire began in 31 BCE, although the Roman Republic was around for hundreds of years before that. The Roman army defeated the Greeks at the Battle of Corinth in 146 BCE.

The Greek Empire fell for a few reasons. Greek city-states all had different types of governments and were always at war with one another. Also, poor people started to rise up against the wealthy. This left Greece so weak that it could not win against a strong enemy like Rome.

The Greeks had a big impact on Roman culture. Even though Greece was now controlled by the Romans, Greek culture and life mostly stayed the same. People in the eastern part of the Roman Empire spoke Greek for hundreds of years after the Romans took over. The Romans believed in many Greek gods, but they changed their names. Zeus became

Jupiter (king of the gods), Ares became Mars (god of war), Aphrodite became Venus (goddess of love and beauty), and Poseidon became Neptune (god of the sea.) But Romans were influential, too. The idea of being "innocent until proven guilty" came from Rome and is still used in many legal systems today.

Romans were amazing builders. They built an enormous amphitheater, called the Colosseum, where people could watch contests between fighters called gladiators. Rome, the empire's capital, had forums in the city center where people traded goods, prayed in temples, voted for leaders, and met friends and family.

Augustus, the first Roman emperor, built huge temples, statues, and pillars in the Roman Forum. He also built long aqueducts for carrying water. The Romans gathered in bathhouses, where they washed and talked to one another in pools of hot water that were like hot tubs or spas.

Roman culture had a huge influence on our world today. From people being "innocent until proven guilty," to large forums where people gather to discuss politics, the foundations of much of modern architecture, sewage systems, and voting rights were built by Romans.

HISTORY REVEALED

In the Greek city-state of Sparta, boys as young as seven went to a military school called the *agoge*. There, they were trained to fight, read, and write, but were not given very much to eat so they would get used to surviving on very little during war. At age 20, they joined the Spartan army.

EXPLORE MORE!

Take a virtual tour around the Colosseum in Rome, Italy, at HistoryView.org or Il-Colosseo.it.

THE CHINESE EMPIRE AND THE INVENTION OF PAPER

Invention of Paper: 105 CE

The Chinese Empire made many contributions to the world. One of the most important Chinese inventions was paper. It was created around 100 CE, when the Han dynasty was ruling. In the beginning, paper was made out of rags. Later, the Chinese began to use tree and plant parts like bark and bamboo. First, two people would cut the bamboo shoots and beat them flat. Then another person would soak the bamboo in water. Finally, someone would tie the flattened, dried bamboo shoots together to make a book.

Paper was in high demand because the national civil servants, or people who worked for the government, had a lot of paperwork to do. The ink they used was in a stick that they mashed against a stone and then dipped in water. They wrote with a type of paintbrush in a method called calligraphy.

The Chinese also wrote on silk. During the Han Dynasty, the Chinese began trading silk with the Western world. The

Silk Road, a path by which silk was traded between countries, went from China to Europe. This 4,000-mile "road" was a system of waterways and roads that stretched from China through Europe, the Middle East, and North Africa. It was very dangerous to travel on the Silk Road, though. On the path, there were thieves and even armies willing to kill for the goods.

Silk was made by silkworms and turned into not only paper but also clothing. People in Europe loved how soft silk was. Silk was especially popular in Rome. Wealthy people liked to wear this fine, smooth fabric. Chinese merchants also sold tea, spices, and jade stones. They got gold, glass, horses, elephants, and wool in exchange for silk. The other big thing brought to China through the Silk Road was religion—Indian merchants introduced the Chinese to Buddhism during the Han Dynasty.

Paper money was also invented in China. It was called "flying money" because it was so light that it could fly away easily. The Chinese made toilet paper, too—a very important invention, indeed! Books, paper, and silk continue to be important to this day. The Chinese changed the way information was recorded and passed down over generations.

HISTORY REVEALED

A court official named Cai Lun is often given credit for inventing paper in 105 CE. However, he only told the emperor about the paper making. Someone made a note of that and it was later misinterpreted that Cai Lun created paper.

EXPLORE MORE!

Read *The Silk Roads: An Illustrated New History of the World* by Peter Frankopan.

THE LIFE OF JESUS

(4 BCE–33 CE)

Jesus (also called Christ, or Jesus Christ) was a Jewish leader whose teachings became the basis for Christianity. Christianity is the most followed religion in the world today.

Most historians believe that Jesus Christ was born in 4 BCE. Jesus believed in one God who was kind and forgiving. Believing in only one god is called "monotheism." His followers, who came to be known as Christians, believe that Jesus is God's son and that his birth by his mother, Mary, was a miracle. Christianity spread throughout the Roman Empire, but Christians were punished for no longer believing in the Roman gods. The rise of Christianity took place from 33 to 300 CE. Jesus taught lessons through parables, or stories that have a meaning behind them. His teachings were always based on love. He is said to have performed many miracles.

Romans were worried that Christians would start to believe their one God was more powerful than the emperor. A Roman governor thought Jesus might get people to fight against the government, so they sentenced him to death. He was hung on a cross in front of lots of people in 33 CE.

Four of Jesus's main followers—Matthew, Mark, Luke, and John—are said to have written down his teachings many years after he died. These four books are known as the Gospels. The Gospels say Jesus was resurrected, or came back to life, to tell his disciples (his students) to spread his teachings. Jesus said that God was good and people needed to be kind to each other in order to live an eternal (forever) life. Another follower, Saul, was Roman and originally Jewish. On the road to Damascus, he saw a blinding light that he believed to be coming down from heaven. He then became known as Saint Paul and began to spread this new religion of Christianity to non-Jews around the eastern Mediterranean. He was killed in Rome around 67 CE.

Christianity grew so much that it became a crime in Rome to believe in Jesus because the Romans were afraid that this belief would stop people from worshipping the Roman gods. People who were persecuted, or killed because they were Christian, are called martyrs. Still, millions of Christians believed in Jesus.

Christianity is the most practiced religion in the world today. More than 2.3 billion people (31 percent of the world's population) practice Christianity and believe in Jesus.

Judeo-Christians once belonged to one group until they split into Judaism and Christianity. Jewish people believe in and pray to God, but not Jesus Christ. Christians believe that God and Jesus are one. They believe in the divine trinity of God, Jesus, and the Holy Spirit.

EXPLORE MORE!

You can learn about Christianity and other religions in *Comparative Religion: Investigate the World through Religious Tradition* by Carla Mooney.

THE PROPHET MUHAMMAD AND THE RISE OF ISLAM

(610–1200)

The Prophet Muhammad was the leader of the Muslim people, who practice a religion called Islam. Muslims believe that Muhammad was the last prophet sent by God to communicate with people. Muslims follow Islam, which is the second most practiced religion in the world today, after Christianity.

Muhammad was born around 570 in the city of Mecca in what is now Saudi Arabia. His family was wealthy and powerful. His parents passed away, so his uncle Abu Talib raised him. Muhammad was a merchant and a shepherd. In 595, when Muhammad was 25, he married a 40-year-old widow (a woman whose husband has died) named Khadijah.

Muhammad used to go into a cave on a mountain near Mecca to meditate and think about life. People believe he was visited by the archangel Gabriel, and got messages from God from 609 to 632. These messages were written down and became the Quran, the main religious book in Islam.

Even today, no matter where they are in the world, Muslims pray in the direction of the Kaaba, which is located in the Grand Mosque of Mecca. In Islam, God is called Allah. There are five pillars of Islam: 1) Faith: There is only one God and Muhammad was God's messenger; 2) Prayer: Muslims pray five times a day facing Mecca; 3) Charity: Every Muslim is supposed to give some of their money to the poor. Muslims who are poor themselves do not have to give; 4) Fasting: During the month of Ramadan, Muslims do not eat from sunrise to sundown in order to strengthen their connection to God; 5) Trip to Mecca: Every Muslim who can afford to, and is physically able, should make a pilgrimage, or long journey, to Mecca at least one time in their life. When they get there, one of the things they do is circle the Kaaba.

Islam is followed all over Asia. It is also a widespread religion in the Arab world, Africa, Europe, and North America. Almost 25 percent of the people on earth practice Islam, which amounts to 1.9 billion people.

HISTORY REVEALED

Although Islam began in Saudi Arabia, which is part of the Arab world, not all Muslims are Arabs. Only about 20 percent of the 1.9 billion Muslims live in the Middle East. Indonesia (in Southeast Asia) has the most Muslim people, and India will likely have more Muslims than any other country by 2050.

EXPLORE MORE!

If you want to read stories about Muhammad, this is a great book: *The Story of the Holy Prophet Muhammad: Ramadan Classics: 30 Stories for 30 Nights* by Humera Malik.

THE CRUSADES

(1095–1291)

During the Middle Ages, there were military missions called Crusades. European Christians went to Jerusalem to take back the Holy Land from Islamic rule. There were eight crusades in all.

The Crusades took place between 1095 and 1291, lasting for almost 200 years! They started because the Pope, who was the leader of the Catholic Church, thought that Christians were not being allowed to make the pilgrimage to Jerusalem. Jerusalem is still a holy city for Muslims, Christians, and Jewish people.

Beginning in the 11th century, the emperor in Constantinople (now called Istanbul and located in modern-day Turkey) asked Christians to fight against Muslims and take over the Holy Land. Knights and monks fought in these bloody battles. Many nobles went off to fight in the Crusades and left their land to the king, so the power of nobles got weaker during this time.

The First Crusade started in the summer of 1096, when 12,000 French peasants and two German armies marched through Europe. This was called the Peasants'

Crusade. One-third of those soldiers died before they even got to Constantinople. Then, later that year, the Nobles' Crusade was led by lords and French warriors. Those French fighters took Jerusalem from the Muslims in 1099. They killed Muslims, Jews, and even some Christians.

The Second Crusade was not so successful. Muslims took back Jerusalem. During the Third Crusade, which started in 1189, the French, Germans, and English fought against the Muslim leader, Saladin. King Richard I of England eventually negotiated an agreement that Christians could go into Jerusalem again. After Saladin died, the Fourth Crusade was organized by Pope Innocent III in 1202. During medieval times, there was a system called feudalism. In it, there were kings, lords, barons, knights, serfs, and peasants. Lords owned land on which serfs and peasants worked. In 1215, King John of England signed the Magna Carta Libertatum ("Great Charter of Freedoms"). This document protected churches' rights, prevented barons from being put in prison illegally, promised a fast trial, and limited payments made to the Crown. But the charter was canceled by Pope Innocent III. Henry III revised and reissued the Magna Carta in 1216.

The Crusades opened Italian port cities to trade. Spices, glass, rugs, jewelry, medicines, new ideas, and technology improved life in Europe. But many people were killed during the Crusades. Also, lots of people began to attack Jews. To this day, there is a long-fought struggle over land in Israel, and the major religions all lay claim to Jerusalem as their holy city—Judaism, Islam, and Christianity.

HISTORY REVEALED

Although the Crusades were violent, sometimes people were nice to each other. When England's King Richard I lost his horse, Saladin's brother sent him a new one!

EXPLORE MORE!

Read the historical novel *The Boy Knight: A Tale of the Crusades* by G. A. Henty for an exciting story that takes place during the Third Crusade.

MONGOLIAN INVASION OF EUROPE

(1220s–1240s)

The Mongol Empire in East Asia invaded Europe during the 13th century. The invasion lasted about 50 years and left more than a hundred thousand people dead. In 1206, a Mongol warlord brought all the Mongol tribes together. They called him the Universal Ruler, or Genghis Khan. Genghis Khan and his soldiers were the strongest army the world had ever known, and they soon set out to take over the continent of Asia. It took them less than 50 years to conquer Asia—a land that stretched from the Pacific Ocean to Eastern Europe.

Some of their tricky tactics were attacking their enemy by riding in on horseback, shooting arrows, and surprising them. Mongols were nomadic, which means that they moved around from place to place. Still, they had camels, sheep, goats, and horses.

Later, in 1398, these warriors took over India's capital city, Delhi, stealing diamonds, rubies, and pearls. They murdered 100,000 Hindus and sold others into slavery. They had powerful cannons (weapons that launched a giant metal ball), which helped them take over many countries. Mongols used other weapons like firebombs, daggers, and liquids that could be lit on fire.

Because the Mongols were taking over much of Eastern Europe, the royalty there decided to work together and fight against them. They stopped all wars among their own countries (but started them again after the Mongols left).

The Mongols even sent spies into Europe before attacking. The spies would tell them how the land was laid out. Then, they invaded with three armies! During this time, Genghis Khan died, and historians think that the Mongols decided that they had to go back to Mongolia to elect a new leader. The empire was split into different territories, each ruled by one of Genghis Khan's sons. These areas are what today we call Eastern China and the city of Beijing, Russia, Central Asia, and Iran. Another theory, or guess, is that the weather got cold and the ground became wet, so the Mongols retreated after defeating Croatia, Hungary, Poland, and much of Eastern Europe. Some people think that the Mongols left because Europeans had more food and bigger horses. It is not known exactly why, but the Mongols stopped their invasion of Europe in the mid-1200s to the early 1300s.

HISTORY REVEALED

Rumors spread across Europe and Asia that the Mongols had been defeated by the German king. German writers said that the Mongols ended their invasion of Europe because of the strong German crusading army. Historians disagree on exactly why the Mongols left Europe but agree that it wasn't because of a military defeat.

EXPLORE MORE!

Look for the historical novel *Daughter of Xanadu* by Dori Jones Yang to read about an adventurous Mongol princess who wants to become a warrior.

BLACK DEATH

(1347–1351)

The Black Death was a deadly disease, or plague, that killed millions of people in Europe.

In the mid-1300s, a deadly bubonic plague spread across Europe and Asia. Twelve "death ships" arrived at the port of Messina, Sicily, in October of 1347. When the merchants docked from sailing on the Black Sea, almost all the sailors on the ships were dead. The ones who were still alive were very sick, their bodies covered with black boils ("buboes"). During the next five years, the Black Death killed more than 20 million Europeans—almost a third of the entire population of Europe.

People believe the Black Death was caused by a kind of bacteria that fleas on rats carry. The bacteria came to Europe when traders returned from other lands. While the European outbreak started in Italy, it soon spread to France, Germany, England, and Russia. By 1351, whole villages in Russia and Eastern Europe were wiped out.

Lots of people thought that God was punishing them. Some wrongly blamed Jewish people, claiming Jews had poisoned the wells and caused the plague. That led to antisemitic attacks against Jewish people, mostly in Germany. Thousands of Jews were killed between 1348 and 1351. Many Jewish people fled to Poland because the Polish king protected them.

Because more than 20 million people in Europe died, there were fewer workers for farming. Those who survived demanded higher pay. Some even begged their landlords to free them from being serfs (servants who worked on a lord's land and were treated like property) and to let them pay rent instead.

Historians disagree about exact numbers but, in Asia, tens of millions were killed by the plague. Across Europe, almost a third of the population died in just four years. People continued to beg forgiveness from God, as they thought they had done something to bring on the terrible suffering that came with this illness.

Both men and women had swellings on their bodies the size of an apple or an egg. Other symptoms included chills, fever, vomiting, diarrhea, awful aches and pains, and, of course, death. The swellings were in the lymph nodes in the neck, under the arms, or near the pelvis. The disease spread into the blood or lungs. Europe eventually slowed the spread by quarantining sailors at port when they arrived.

The world is experiencing another global pandemic, COVID-19. Although modern medicine has improved a lot since this early plague, people tend to learn from the mistakes that transpired long ago. The idea of quarantining ships at port or people in their homes started during the Black Death pandemic and has helped keep many people safer during COVID-19.

HISTORY REVEALED

People used to think that the Black Death could be spread if others just looked at them. Modern science now knows that some diseases caused by viruses and bacteria are airborne, which means they are spread when someone breathes the same air that a sick person does.

EXPLORE MORE!

Visit KidsHealth.org/kids for lots of tips on staying healthy, like how to wash your hands to prevent the spread of germs.

THE RENAISSANCE

(1300s–1600s)

After the terrible events of the Black Death, a "rebirth," or renaissance, began in Italy. The Renaissance was a period when art, science, philosophy, and literature moved to the forefront of life. During the 16th century, the Renaissance spread from Italy to other parts of Europe.

Among the many people who made a significant contribution to the Renaissance was Leonardo da Vinci. Perhaps the most famous artist of this time, da Vinci was an inventor, engineer, scientist, and painter. He studied the human body and came up with ideas for inventions, including flying machines. In the early 1500s, he painted the *Mona Lisa*, now one of the most famous paintings in the world.

In 1508, Michelangelo, another Renaissance artist, began painting the massive ceiling of the Sistine Chapel in Rome. Standing on scaffolding, he created a series of frescoes (paintings done on wet plaster) of God with angels and people. This masterpiece took him four years to complete. Michelangelo also sculpted the magnificent marble statue *David*.

Many new scientific ideas emerged during the Renaissance. In the early 1500s, mathematician and astronomer Nicolaus

Copernicus proposed that the Sun was at the center of the solar system. Later, astronomer Galileo suggested that the Moon might rotate on its axis. This helped prove that Earth and other planets revolve around the Sun and the Moon moves around Earth. The Catholic Church was upset when Galileo discovered this because it meant Earth was not the center of the universe.

During the Renaissance, architecture—the design and construction of buildings—changed a lot. Architect Filippo Brunelleschi showed how drawing two lines coming closer together could make things look as if they were far apart. This is called "linear perspective." Brunelleschi designed the dome of the Florence Cathedral, still the largest brick dome in the world.

Literature of this period often focused on describing people and nature as they really are. Poet Francesco Petrarca wrote sonnets (14-line poems) about feelings and nature. In England, playwright William Shakespeare wrote about love, ambition, and other human emotions. Many of his plays, such as *Romeo and Juliet* and *Hamlet*, are still performed all over the world.

The Renaissance was a period rich with discoveries and ideas. Much of our modern literature, art, and architecture are based on the developments that occurred during this time.

HISTORY REVEALED

Leonardo da Vinci may be one of the most famous painters of all time, but he was also known for starting projects and never finishing them. He got easily distracted by his immense curiosity and was not able to focus for long enough to finish paintings, even some that he was already paid to do!

EXPLORE MORE!

Read *A Stage Full of Shakespeare Stories* by Angela McAllister for illustrated retellings of 12 Shakespeare plays, written just for kids.

THE HUNDRED YEARS' WAR

(1337–1453)

E ngland and France fought a long war on and off for 100 years. It was a fight over land, power, and who would take control of the throne.

The Hundred Years' War started because the English royal family was originally French. So English monarchs owned land in France. Sometimes English monarchs held more land in France than the French royals themselves. During the Middle Ages, French monarchs tried to stop the spread of English power, taking away their land whenever they could. They did this especially when England fought Scotland, an ally, or friend, of France.

Then, in 1328, the French king Charles IV died. Charles's sister, Isabella of France, was his closest living relative. Isabella tried to claim the throne for her son Edward III of England, but French barons said she could not do this. They said that because she was a woman, she could not inherit a kingdom. They also probably did not want an English king.

When France invaded the coast of England, Edward gathered an army and declared war.

The fighting between the two countries continued off and on for years, with England losing much of its French land. But in 1415, King Henry V of England invaded France and won an amazing victory at the Battle of Agincourt against a French army much larger than England's. A few years later, Henry invaded Paris, and the French then named him as leader of their country.

In 1429, a young girl named Joan of Arc talked the French king's son Charles VII into fighting back against England. She claimed that the saints spoke to her. Joan of Arc was captured, called crazy, tried in court, found guilty, and burned at the stake! But Charles VII managed to win back much of France, and, by 1453 England had run out of money. That brought the Hundred Years' War to an end.

The Hundred Years' War was one of one of the biggest conflicts of the Middle Ages, fought by five generations of kings who dueled over the right to rule France. In 1453, the French won; however, for a hundred years, people spent their whole lives at war. Generations of families only knew this long-standing fight. In the end, France and England's borders and countries were stronger and more defined. Even after the war ended, competition between the French and English kept going and influenced how those two countries would take over other parts of the world later on.

HISTORY REVEALED

Joan of Arc was thought to be possessed, or controlled by an evil power, because she said she heard voices. Doctors now think that she might have had a mental illness like schizophrenia, or a physical condition such as epilepsy. She could also simply have had bad headaches (called migraines) or an illness that you get from drinking unpasteurized milk.

EXPLORE MORE!

Read *Strong Girls in History* by Susan B. Katz to learn about Joan of Arc and 14 other amazing young women.

THE INVENTION OF THE PRINTING PRESS

(1440s)

A printing press is a machine that places letters on paper to make books. It was invented in the early 1400s, although similar inventions had been used earlier in China and Korea.

A goldsmith from Germany named Johannes Gutenberg, who was sent to France in exile, is given credit for inventing the printing press in the 1400s. However, Chinese and Korean bookmakers used woodblock printing as early as the 9th century.

At that time in China, there were also printed calendars, math charts, a dictionary, and schoolbooks. Bi Sheng, a Chinese inventor (970–1051 CE), made the first moveable type by carving letters in clay and baking them into hard blocks. Those blocks were then placed on an iron frame that was pushed up against an iron plate.

Still, Gutenberg invented the first "modern" printed book in Europe in 1455. He made movable type (letters on metal that could print over and over). This opened up the possibility of people sharing more information with each other. Books were printed in Latin and Greek. Gutenberg's first book was the Bible translated into Latin. Researchers think that he printed 200 copies of this 1,300-page Bible.

Before the printing press was invented, people had to copy books by hand or retell stories orally. The main difference between Gutenberg's design and the Chinese printing style was that Gutenberg used metal instead of wood. Gutenberg put the letters backward, in brass. He put the letters together in several straight lines and columns on flat paper.

Gutenberg also made his own ink, a special formula that would stick to metal. He flattened the paper he printed on by using a winepress, which was used to smash grapes for wine and press olives for oil. He made that technology work for his printing press design.

It's fair to say that you might not be reading this book right now were it not for Gutenberg's printing press invention. Books made people's ability to share information, and stories, possible. Imagine what the world would be like without books. Gutenberg planted the seed from which books were born.

HISTORY REVEALED

Even though Gutenberg made this important invention, he died penniless. The people who gave him the money to build the printing press took it back. He printed 200 copies of the Bible, but only three people could read it in Latin. He couldn't sell the other 197 copies.

EXPLORE MORE!

Look for *Creative Paper Crafts: 35 Cool, Customizable Projects for Crafty Kids* by Lisa Glover to have fun making art out of paper.

THE SPANISH INQUISITION

(1478–1834)

During the Spanish Inquisition, the king and queen of Spain ordered Jewish and Muslim people to either convert to Christianity or leave their country. If they lied about converting, they were tortured and killed.

There are many theories, or educated guesses, as to why the Spanish Inquisition started. One theory is that King Ferdinand and Queen Isabella of Spain felt like there were too many religions in their country. Another idea is that the rulers of Spain wanted to make their country, and the Catholic Church, stronger. So in 1478, they began an inquisition, which is something like a harsh questioning. Their idea was to get rid of people who did not follow Christianity or Catholicism, especially Jewish and Muslim people. In 1492 and 1502, two royal decrees ordered all Muslims and Jews to either convert to Catholicism or leave Spain.

In 1492, the Spanish army took over Granada, which was the last Spanish city where Muslims had control. Some converts, or *conversos*, said they had converted but secretly practiced their own religion at home. They were often turned in by their neighbors and pressured to confess.

During the Inquisition, Tomás de Torquemada was in charge. He ordered books to be burned, including the most sacred Jewish writings, called the Talmud. Tomás also demanded that thousands of Muslim manuscripts, written in the Arabic language, be burned.

The inquisition itself was like a court that questioned people who claimed to be converts to Catholicism and punished those they thought were still practicing other religions. The first execution, or killing, is thought to have taken place in the Spanish city of Seville on February 6, 1481. From there, the Inquisition progressed quickly. The Spanish tortured and expelled, or kicked out, more than 150,000 people and burned thousands at the stake.

The Inquisition did not formally end until 1834, when Isabella II was in power. It is believed that of the 80,000 Jews in Spain, only about 40,000 fled. Most of the others chose to convert to Catholicism.

The world looks back on events like the Spanish Inquisition and sees them as something that could never happen today; however, people are still treated unfairly based on their religion in modern times.

HISTORY REVEALED

Many Jewish people have Ladino lineage, or Sephardic roots, meaning that their ancestors came from Spain during the Spanish Inquisition and went to North Africa, later ending up in Eastern Europe and the Middle East.

EXPLORE MORE!

Look for *World History: 500 Facts* by Brooke Khan to find fascinating information about the Spanish Inquisition and hundreds of other events in world history.

PORTUGAL SETS SAIL

(1400s–1504)

Portuguese sailors set out on the Atlantic Ocean in the early 1400s under the direction of Prince Henry. This was the beginning of the Age of Exploration. Prince Henry wanted to find a route to Asia where spices and jewels could be found.

In 1415, Prince Henry, along with his father and brothers, took over Ceuta, a Muslim city in North Africa that was rich from trading. The Portuguese got maps of Africa to explore more, and Henry opened a mapmaking school in Lisbon, Portugal. The prince hired men who sailed down the west coast of Africa, in ships he owned, to expand trade for Portugal. Henry's sailors also brought back African people, whom they later enslaved. While this was the beginning of the Age of Exploration, Portuguese explorers also started the devastating European slave trade.

Pirates often captured Portuguese ships, and Prince Henry wanted to stop this. He created a new type of ship, called a caravel. It was lighter than other ships and could sail farther and faster. It also could sail "into the wind" and did not need to go in the direction the wind was blowing. Another Portuguese discovery was the *volta do mar*, or "turn of the sea." This was a wind pattern that helped them on their trips to and from Africa. Going south, they would sail along the coast. On the way back, they would sail far west into the ocean to catch the winds that blew them back.

In 1488, the Portuguese explorer Bartolomeu Dias sailed from Portugal to the southernmost point of Africa and went around the Cape of Good Hope. Then, in 1497, Vasco da Gama made it all the way around Africa and reached the Indian Ocean. Da Gama got to Calicut, India, where the locals had spices. He went back four times to get more goods to trade. In 1512, the Portuguese landed on the Spice Islands in Indonesia for the first time. The Portuguese helped Europe expand and explore, connecting with other continents and countries. The new trade routes opened up people's worlds, added spices to their food, introduced them to new kinds of fabrics, and expanded their ability to make money. But the Portuguese also captured and enslaved African people.

The Age of Exploration started with Portugal's voyages to new lands and changed the course of history. The way in which explorers conquered civilizations, enslaved African people, and claimed territory led to wars in the United States, Europe, and Africa.

HISTORY REVEALED

Around 600 CE, long before the European slave trade, Arab Muslims put enslaved Africans in ships with the gold and salt that they traded. Slavery was a business transaction for much of history, and it took a grave toll on the lives of enslaved people and their descendants (children, grandchildren, etc.).

EXPLORE MORE!

Read *The World Made New: Why the Age of Exploration Happened and How It Changed the World* by Marc Aronson and John W. Glenn to learn more about this extraordinary time in world history.

COLUMBUS EXPLORES THE AMERICAS

(1492–1504)

Christopher Columbus was an Italian explorer, but he sailed under the Spanish flag. Queen Isabella I and King Ferdinand II paid him to explore for the Spanish. He made four trips between 1492 and 1504. Columbus is most known for "discovering" the Americas because for a long time he was believed to be the first European to arrive there. However, Native American, or Indigenous, people already lived in North and South America.

In 1492, Columbus sailed from Spain, heading west. He had three ships—the *Niña*, the *Pinta*, and the *Santa María*. His goal was to get to Asia by going west from Spain. He was looking for gold and spices because he wanted to get rich. On his first voyage, he landed in the Bahamas, a chain of islands about 50 miles (80 kilometers) from the coast of modern-day Florida. Because he was looking for India, he called this area the West Indies. He thought that he had reached India, and called the people there *Indios*. This is why Native Americans used to be called Indians.

Columbus then went to the islands of Cuba and Hispaniola. He created a colony in what is now Haiti. When he went back to Spain in 1493, he brought dozens of Indigenous people as captured prisoners. His next trips to the New World were to the Lesser Antilles in 1493, Trinidad and South America in 1498, and Central America in 1502. He never reached North America.

Columbus and his crew brought deadly diseases like chickenpox and measles to the Americas. Also, recent findings show how he and the European explorers who followed him beat, enslaved, and killed millions of Indigenous people. Cities around the world have replaced Columbus Day with Indigenous Peoples' Day to honor the Native Americans who were wiped out.

Columbus's exploration and colonization changed the Western world as we know it. His trips paved the way for more colonization, and the trade routes he established altered the course of history. They were, in many ways, the stepping-stones to enslaved people being brought to the Americas.

HISTORY REVEALED

Columbus first asked Portugal to sponsor, or pay for, his trip. When they said no, he went to his homeland of Italy. They, too, declined, so he asked the king and queen of Spain and they said yes.

EXPLORE MORE!

Read *Encounter*, written by Jane Yolen and illustrated by David Shannon, for a tale about Christopher Columbus told from the perspective of a boy on the island of San Salvador, one of the places Columbus landed in 1492.

CORTÉS AND SOUTH AMERICAN AZTECS

(1519–1521)

Hernán Cortés was a Spanish explorer who came to Mexico and destroyed almost the entire population of Aztec people.

The Spanish explorer Hernán Cortés sailed from Cuba to Mexico 500 years ago—almost 30 years after Columbus's expeditions. He wanted to colonize Mexico's Aztec people and convert them to Catholicism. Cortés first befriended the Aztecs to gain their trust. He had only 600 men with him when he landed in Mexico in 1519. The Aztec emperor, Montezuma II, welcomed them. The Aztecs had not seen horses or armor before. They thought that Cortés was a god named Quetzalcóatl (ket-zal-COAT-ill).

In 1519, Cortés captured Montezuma as his prisoner with the help of some of the tribes that were at war with the Aztecs. In 1521, Cortés also captured the capital city of Tenochtitlán and claimed the Aztec empire for Spain.

Tens of thousands of Aztecs were wiped out, mostly by diseases Cortés and his men brought, like smallpox. The capital had roughly 200,000 people when Cortés and his army came. Disease killed almost half of them.

Smallpox was a virus to which the Aztecs had never been exposed. One monk who traveled with Cortés said, "In many places it happened that everyone in a house died, and as it was impossible to bury the great number of dead, they pulled down the houses over them, so that their homes became their tombs." The smallpox outbreak went on for 70 days, and about one out of three people who caught it died. It was not only the Aztecs who suffered with smallpox; the Mayan and Incan civilizations were also devastated. It wasn't until 1796 that a smallpox vaccine was developed.

Aztec, Mayan, and Incan culture are the backbone of civilization in Mexico, Central America, and South America. Many of the traditions, ancient ruins, and original languages of the Aztec and Mayan people are honored today, despite the entire population almost getting wiped out. Also, Cortés and his troops caused millions of people to convert to Catholicism. Most Mexicans, and people in Latin America in general, now practice this religion. Some Indigenous people still follow their ancestral traditions and worship ancient gods, though.

HISTORY REVEALED

Modern-day Mexico City was built on top of ruins like the Templo Mayor (Tenochtitlán's main temple). These ancient, sacred grounds were not uncovered until 1978!

EXPLORE MORE!

The Aztec civilization left behind many extraordinary sculptures made of stone. One of the most famous is a statue of the goddess Coatlicue (koh-at-LEE-kway). The statue is more than 10 feet tall and shows the goddess wearing a skirt of snakes. You can see photographs and learn more about it at SmartHistory.org/coatlicue.

THE TRANSATLANTIC SLAVE TRADE

(1500s–1800s)

Europeans began enslaving people from West Africa in the mid-1500s. The slave trade devastated millions of people's lives as they were brought, against their will, to the United States, Caribbean, and Brazil.

African kingdoms with rich cultural traditions existed before and after Europeans enslaved people on the African continent. Europeans chained and shackled African people and forced them onto ships with very unhealthy, unlivable conditions. Millions of Africans died on the way to the Americas and many others arrived very ill. The ones who survived were sold at auctions, then forced to work as free laborers. They got beaten, mistreated, and even killed.

Between 1525 and 1866, about 12.5 million enslaved people were taken from Africa to Europe, the Caribbean, North America, and South America. Only 10.7 million survived the Middle Passage over the Atlantic Ocean from Africa to the New World. Of those, about 388,000 were brought by force to North America.

The slave ships sailed from European ports filled with textiles, wine, guns, and iron. When they reached West Africa, the goods were exchanged, as a business, for people who were taken into slavery. This was called the Triangular Trade because it involved three lands: Britain, Africa, and the Caribbean. By 1780, between 80,000 and 100,000 enslaved Africans were brought to the Americas each year. Many families were separated and never saw each other again. Children were even ripped from their mother's arms!

For hundreds of years, abolitionists in the United States fought to end slavery. Brave Black leaders like Frederick Douglass, Sojourner Truth, and Harriet Tubman led this historic movement to end the slave trade and free people from slavery. The Underground Railroad was formed, through which people like Harriet Tubman led enslaved people north to freedom.

The institution of slavery continued in the United States for more than 300 years. The Southern states wanted to keep slavery because they depended on it to gain wealth through the production of food and cotton. This led to a battle between the Northern and Southern states, called the Civil War.

Eventually, slavery in the United States was abolished, or made illegal, with the adoption of the 13th Amendment to the US Constitution in 1865.

HISTORY REVEALED

In 2019, a slave ship called the *Clotilda* was discovered. It smuggled 109 enslaved Africans up through the Mobile River in Alabama, in 1860, more than 50 years after bringing enslaved people to the United States was made illegal. The *Clotilda* captives were the last of about 388,000 enslaved Africans brought to North America.

EXPLORE MORE!

Two books about slavery you might want to read are *Show Way* by Jacqueline Woodson, illustrated by Hudson Talbott, and *Copper Sun* by Sharon M. Draper.

THE SEVEN YEARS' WAR

(1756–1763)

The Seven Years' War was the first global battle. It was a fight among many European countries over land, trade routes, and control of crucial ports.

The Seven Years' War began in Europe, where Prussians (people from the German state of Prussia, which no longer exists) were fighting against the Austrians over control of a piece of land in central Europe called Silesia. Britain started backing Prussia, and France supported Austria, but France and England soon turned their attention to their territories in India and North America.

England and France became the main colonizers in North America. They fought for nine years (not seven) over control of the fur trade in the Ohio River Valley and Gulf of St. Lawrence in Canada. It became known as the Seven Years' War (1756–1763), but the fight between Great Britain and France started earlier, in 1754. Moving furs on these water-ways was very important, because it was a main source of income, and the British felt like French trade was stopping their expansion. Spain became involved in the war in 1761 and was aligned with France. That ended up being a very bad move for Spain, because they later lost two major ports to Britain: Havana, Cuba, and Manila, Philippines. The Caribbean Islands were a big source of sugar, so losing Havana hit Spain hard.

But the French and British did not fight alone against each other. Native Americans from the Huron tribe taught the French guerrilla warfare, in which they stole supplies and carried out surprise attacks. People from the Iroquois tribes worked with the English army because they were angry at French leaders like Samuel de Champlain. He had killed many Iroquois chiefs. The Iroquois built amazing canoes and long, narrow buildings called longhouses, where many families lived together. They were great traders and had a well-developed government.

George Washington, who later became the first president of the United States, fought with the English army, using guerrilla tactics to beat the French. The powerful English navy, led by the British prime minister, William Pitt the Elder, helped defeat the French.

The war ended in 1763 with the Treaty of Paris, in which the French gave up control of Canada and everywhere east of the Mississippi River. England took over these lands. Spain also gave Florida over to Britain. This was an important turning point in history since the British now had control of most of North America. Eventually, the British clashed with Americans over control of the United States in the Revolutionary War.

HISTORY REVEALED

After all North American territories were divided between the British, French, and Spanish, Native Americans reclaimed seven of the forts the British took. Pontiac's War broke out between a group of Indigenous people, led by the Ottawa chief Pontiac, and the British. The British did not return any of the land to the Native Americans.

EXPLORE MORE!

Read *Birchbark Brigade: A Fur Trade History* by Cris Peterson to learn more about the fur trade in North America.

THE EUROPEAN ENLIGHTENMENT

(1600–1800)

The Age of Enlightenment, also known as the Age of Reason, occurred when people stopped believing only in religion and superstition and started discovering more about reason and science.

The words "I think, therefore I am" were first said by French philosopher René Descartes in 1637. This phrase is considered by some to be the basis of the Enlightenment. People wanted to learn, be free, and pursue happiness.

Ideas about politics and people's rights came out during this time as well. Voltaire, a French philosopher, writer, and historian, challenged the religions of the time, particularly the Roman Catholic Church. He was an advocate, or supporter, of freedom of speech and freedom of religion. He believed the church had too much control over people's lives. Voltaire helped create what we now know as the separation of church and state.

The Scientific Revolution took place during the Enlightenment as new ideas in science were developed, including in mathematics, astronomy, physics, and biology. This revolution led people to believe that reason and science would help them understand the world, and themselves, better.

People started thinking and talking about psychology, or the study of the human mind. John Locke, an English philosopher and physician, suggested that the human mind is a tabula rasa (a "clean slate") when we are born. He claimed that all knowledge comes from personal experiences and these experiences form a person's personality and character during their life. Therefore, a person is not born good or bad.

In the late 1600s, Isaac Newton, an English mathematician and physicist, built on the work done during the Renaissance by Copernicus and Galileo. They established that the Sun, not Earth, was at the center of the solar system. Newton developed math equations that showed how the planets moved in the solar system. He also published a book about gravity, the force that pulls people and objects toward the center of Earth. In 1705, Newton was knighted by Queen Anne and became Sir Isaac Newton.

The challenges to what people used to simply accept as being right, or correct, encouraged people to think for themselves during this time. The idea that people can listen to science and reason, not only religion and rulers, dramatically shifted our world, and how we view it, in a new direction.

Locke wrote a book about people having the right to life, liberty, and property. His thoughts formed the basis of what later became the US Declaration of Independence. Thomas Jefferson admired Locke and wanted his words included, but the wording was changed to "life, liberty, and the pursuit of happiness."

EXPLORE MORE!

Galileo's findings are fascinating. Read more about them in *Starry Messenger* by Peter Sís.

AMERICAN REVOLUTION

(1775–1781)

The American Revolution took place when the 13 British colonies in North America rebelled against Great Britain. The colonies won their independence and formed a new nation: the United States of America.

In the 1760s, people living in the British colonies all along the east coast of North America were not represented in the British government, or Parliament. When Britain told them to pay taxes, they refused and fought to become independent.

The original 13 colonies were founded between 1607 and 1732. In 1764, the British made the Sugar Act, and then the Stamp Act, which were taxes they demanded the colonies pay. In 1770, British soldiers killed five protesters when the colonists were rallying against the British taxes. This was called the Boston Massacre. Then, in 1773, colonists poured expensive tea into Boston Harbor during the Boston Tea Party to protest, or speak out against, taxes on British tea.

In April 1775, Paul Revere made his famous "midnight ride" to let the colonists know the British were about to attack.

He and others rode on horseback, yelling, "The Regulars are coming out!" (Regulars were the British soldiers.)

The colonists met at a Continental Congress where, in June of 1775, George Washington organized the Continental Army. On April 18 and 19, 1775, at the Battles of Lexington and Concord, American colonists defeated the British. They later lost to them at Bunker Hill. England's King George III said the colonist "rebels" were going against British rule.

In response to that, Thomas Jefferson, who went on to become the third president of the United States, drafted the Declaration of Independence. It states, "We hold these truths to be self-evident, that all men are created equal." On July 4, 1776, the Declaration of Independence was signed.

In 1777, the French joined the Americans to defeat the British. Spain followed soon after. With help from Spain and the Dutch Republic (now known as the Netherlands), the colonists beat the British in the Battle of Yorktown, the final fight of the American Revolution in 1781.

Also in 1777, the Articles of Confederation were written by the colonies, but they gave too much power to states and too little to the federal government. So in 1787, the Constitution was created, which laid out the laws of the United States. The Constitution is still what we uphold today, although there have been amendments along the way to allow for more equal rights.

HISTORY REVEALED

In truth, Paul Revere didn't ride alone. More members of the Sons of Liberty, including William Dawes and Dr. Samuel Prescott, warned of the British invasion. But their last names don't rhyme with as much as Revere does, so the poet Henry Wadsworth Longfellow didn't feature them in the poem he wrote about the famous ride.

EXPLORE MORE!

You can learn more about Paul Revere's ride here: *Paul Revere's Ride* by Henry Wadsworth Longfellow, adapted by Ted Rand.

FRENCH REVOLUTION

(1789–1799)

After the French fought in the American Revolution, they too wanted to overthrow their government to gain more rights. The poor were being forced to pay taxes, but the rich nobles were not. Craftspeople, peasants, and the middle class wanted a democracy, not a monarchy that put one king in charge.

In 1787 and 1788, the king, queen, clergy, and wealthy aristocracy lived in luxury, but there weren't enough crops produced to feed the people of France. The country was broke. The price of food rose and the number of jobs dropped. Even with all this hardship, King Louis XVI and his wife, Marie Antoinette, kept having fancy dinners and parties. The Third Estate, or lowest class, were so fed up that in June 1789 they formed the National Assembly.

The king told clergy and nobles to join the new assembly, but, at the same time, he gathered troops to tear it apart. French people heard a rumor that the king was about to do away with the National Assembly, so they rioted. On July 14, 1789, 600 French people took over the Bastille prison looking for weapons. They tore the Bastille apart brick by brick.

July 14th is now known in France as Bastille Day, the equivalent of the United States' Independence Day on July 4th—they have fireworks, too!

This new national assembly took over and made laws similar to those of the United States' democracy. They wrote the Declaration of the Rights of Man and of the Citizen, a document that declared people should have the right to "liberty, property, security, and resistance to oppression." It is very similar to the American Declaration of Independence.

In 1791, France created a new constitution that limited the king's power and gave more influence to a group of politicians that would make the laws. Still, the new government allowed only men over 25 who paid certain taxes to vote, so it was not yet fair to everyone. Things were still unstable in France. People wanted to get rid of the monarchy and not have a king in charge. In 1793, the Reign of Terror began and lasted a year. Tens of thousands of people considered "enemies of the Revolution," including Marie Antoinette, died. Many were beheaded or shot in public.

An army hero named Napoleon Bonaparte started a new government in 1799, ending the French Revolution. After five years in charge, Napoleon declared himself Emperor of France. This led to the Napoleonic Wars, which raged from 1803 to 1815. Eventually, France became a democracy.

HISTORY REVEALED

Napoleon Bonaparte expanded France's empire, invading Italy, Germany, Egypt, and Switzerland, but his troops froze in Russia and retreated. Napoleon was eventually exiled from France but snuck back in and later got defeated. Even after all that struggle under his rule, France still did not have a democracy.

EXPLORE MORE!

Read about the March on Versailles, where 7,000 market women walked 12 miles (19 kilometers), stormed the government palace, and demanded bread for their hungry families, in *Moms Needed Bread! The Women's March on Versailles* by Baby Professor.

HAITIAN REVOLUTION

(1791–1804)

Enslaved Haitians were inspired by the French Revolution to fight for independence. Their leader, Toussaint Louverture, helped Haiti become the first Black-led state in the New World.

The Haitian Revolution was a long time coming. In December 1492, Columbus stumbled upon the island he called La Isla Española, or "the Spanish Island"—Hispaniola in English—which is now Haiti and the Dominican Republic. The Spanish immediately enslaved many native Taino and Ciboney people and forced them to mine gold. The Taino and Ciboney were wiped out by diseases brought in from Europeans and died working in awful conditions in the mines. By the 16th century, almost none of the Taino or Ciboney were left. The Spanish brought thousands more enslaved Africans from other islands, who died in much the same way.

When there was no gold left in the mines, the Spanish left and the French settled on the island in 1665, calling their colony Saint-Domingue. By 1789, just before the French

Revolution began, this colony had 500,000 enslaved Africans, 32,000 Europeans, and 24,000 *affranchis* (people with both African and European backgrounds).

Haitian society was split apart by class, color, and gender. Some of the affranchis were slave owners and tried to become wealthy like the Europeans. The white Europeans were landowners, crafts-people, and merchants. Most of the enslaved population had been born in Africa. They plowed the fields, worked as servants, and a few were even slave drivers. Enslaved people spent very long days doing backbreaking work. They suffered from infections, diseases, and injuries. Many starved to death. A group of enslaved people escaped into the mountains. Their group, called Maroons, fought against the colonial army.

In May 1791, France made the wealthier affranchi citizens, but Europeans in Haiti did not recognize them as equals. Two months later, battles broke out between the affranchis and the French. By August, a rebellion of thousands of enslaved people began. Again, in April 1792, the French gave citizenship to the affranchis, but that did not end the violence. In 1793, Léger-Félicité Sonthonax came from France and abolished, or did away with, slavery.

On January 1, 1804, the western side of Hispaniola, now called Haiti, declared itself free from French rule. This made Haiti the very first independent state in the Americas founded by formerly enslaved people. It was led by Jean-Jacques Dessalines, who had been a key player in the Haitian Revolution.

HISTORY REVEALED

Although slavery in Haiti did not end until 1804, slave rebellions started before 1791. Enslaved people were treated so brutally that they plotted to poison their masters.

EXPLORE MORE!

These books will give you a bigger picture of the Haitian Revolution: *Toussaint Louverture: The Fight for Haiti's Freedom* by Walter Dean Myers, illustrated by Jacob Lawrence, and *Freedom Soup* by Tami Charles, illustrated by Jacqueline Alcántara.

INVENTION OF THE STEAM LOCOMOTIVE

(1804–1900)

Steam trains transformed how goods and people moved about the country and the world. The invention of the steam locomotive opened up more trading opportunities globally.

As far back as 200 BCE, the Greek inventor Hero of Alexandria wrote about an aeolipile, which many think was the first steam engine. A ball with water in it was placed over a pot. When it heated up, two tubes let out steam, which made the ball spin. Much later, in 1712, Thomas Newcomen and John Calley, his assistant, showcased the first steam engine for commercial use.

In the late 1700s, the "father of the steam engine," James Watt, improved the steam engine so it needed less coal to run. Matthew Boulton helped him manufacture these steam engines. Their invention helped start the Industrial Revolution, a time when the main source of work and money changed from products made by hand to goods made in factories by machines. The Industrial Revolution began in Britain and spread around the world.

Between 1802 and 1804, Richard Trevithick, an engineer from England, invented a high-pressure steam locomotive on wheels that could pull heavier loads than horses could. This locomotive was designed to ride on roads, not railways. George Stephenson built the first traveling engine in 1814. It was used to haul coal out of mines. In 1829, George and his son Robert invented the famous Rocket locomotive. People began building railways, and they could now ship goods much faster than ever before. Thousands of people gathered to watch the Rocket get up to 36 miles (58 kilometers) per hour and win a prize (about $61,000 in US dollars today).

Trains carrying goods throughout the world changed how quickly and easily people could receive food, medical supplies, and materials for producing other items to sell. In Britain, the first steam locomotive railroad was the Stockton and Darlington. It was 26 miles (40 kilometers) long and took coal to cargo boats.

Peter Cooper invented the Tom Thumb train in 1830, which carried passengers on the railroad. People no longer had to travel by horse-drawn buggy or boat. This made transportation on land easier and led to railroads being built across the country and the world. Factories no longer had to be located near rivers. Trains became the fastest way to get from place to place. Steam-powered locomotives changed life in the 19th century.

HISTORY REVEALED

Some people feared that women's bodies were "not designed to go 50 miles an hour." They worried that women's uteruses (where babies are carried before they're born) would "fly out of [their] bodies at that speed." Other people thought that the human body might melt on high-speed trains. None of that was true.

EXPLORE MORE!

You can read more about the early invention of steam locomotives and even take a train trip in *Locomotive* by Brian Floca.

THE WOMEN'S MOVEMENT

late 1800s–early 1900s

The women's movement was a time when women fought for equal rights like the right to vote, equal pay, and the ability to own property. As a result of these marches, speeches, and pioneering women, new laws were passed that made many changes toward equality between men and women.

Back in the 1800s, women did not have many, or sometimes any, rights. When the Industrial Revolution began, more workers were needed and women got factory jobs and worked as salesclerks, secretaries, or typists. Other women became nurses or teachers. By the 1830s, women in the United States and Europe wanted to own property, go to university, work any job they chose, and be able to get a divorce. Feminism, the idea that women and men should have equal rights, began and the women's movement built up momentum.

Susan B. Anthony and Elizabeth Cady Stanton gave speeches about, and fought for, women's rights in the United States. In 1848, at the Seneca Falls Convention, Stanton spoke about the Declaration of Rights and Sentiments, which she wrote based on the Declaration of Independence. This document was signed by 68 women and 32 men, including Frederick Douglass. It declared that women and men are equal and should have equal rights.

The right to vote (also called suffrage) was also important to women. People who fought for women's suffrage were called suffragists. In the early 1900s, the suffragists in England protested by going on hunger strikes (which means refusing to eat) and chaining themselves to the prime minister of England's house.

In 1893, New Zealand was the first country to give all women the right to vote. Wyoming became the first US territory to grant women the right to vote in 1869. Australia followed in 1902; Finland in 1906; and Norway in 1913. Finally, in 1920, only about 100 years ago, the 19th Amendment to the Constitution gave women the right to vote across the United States. Shortly after that, in 1928, women over the age of 21 became eligible to vote in Britain.

In many places, women are still not allowed to drive, own property, or attend school, and are sometimes paid much less than men for the same job. Suffragists and other activists paved the path for generations of girls and women who came after them. March has been declared Women's History Month, during which people learn about pioneers like pilot Amelia Earhart or Rebecca Lee Crumpler, the first African American woman to become a doctor.

HISTORY REVEALED

The 19th Amendment didn't give all women the right to vote. It actually says, "The right of citizens of the United States to vote shall not be denied or abridged by the United States or by any State on account of sex." So it made voting discrimination illegal based on someone's sex, not their race. Black women still didn't have the right to vote until almost 50 years later.

EXPLORE MORE!

Read *Bold Women in History: 15 Women's Rights Activists You Should Know* by Meghan Vestal to learn more about Susan B. Anthony, Elizabeth Cady Stanton, and other important people in feminist history.

GOLD RUSH

1848–1855

The Gold Rush began when people discovered gold in the American West, inspiring prospectors from around the globe to rush to the rivers of California and mine for gold. This meant that cities like San Francisco were built up almost overnight.

In 1848, James Marshall was building a sawmill in California for a Swiss man named John Sutter. While digging near a river, James discovered a small piece of gold. Soon, word spread about the gold in California. One merchant, Samuel Brannan, ran through the streets of San Francisco shouting, "Gold! Gold! Gold from the American River!" Within two years, tens of thousands of people from all over the world came to claim some gold for themselves. These gold seekers were called "forty-niners" because the height of the gold rush was in 1849. At first people panned for gold in rivers by shaking out a tray of water, rocks, and soil to find gold nuggets. Later, new technology allowed mines to be built, which made it easier to prospect, or search, for gold.

Half of the people coming to California arrived by boat from Asia, Europe, and Latin America. The other half traveled across the country on foot or by ox-drawn carriage. San Francisco, the closest settlement to Gold Country at the time, went from a population of 200 people in 1846 to a booming 36,000 in 1852. In 1849 alone, an estimated 90,000 gold seekers came to California. Of those, about 50,000 to 60,000 came from across North America. The others hailed from foreign lands.

Sadly, the rapid immigration of forty-niners meant that Indigenous people in the area were killed by disease, starvation, and the California Genocide (the killing of thousands of Indigenous people). Gold miners killed Indigenous people in large numbers so they could take their land. Europeans and North Americans also captured and enslaved Indigenous people to work in the gold mines.

By 1850, most of the gold had been mined and Americans tried to kick foreigners out of the country. They charged a monthly fee of $20 (which is about $700 in 2021) and began attacking miners from China and Latin America. Indigenous people fought to maintain their land and bloody battles broke out between American prospectors and Indigenous tribes.

Much of the development of the San Francisco Bay Area is due to the Gold Rush. It is still important for international shipping and trade today. Gold continues to be one of the most valuable metals in the world.

HISTORY REVEALED

Another result of the Gold Rush is Levi's jeans! A businessman named Levi Strauss started selling jean overalls to miners in San Francisco in 1853. Levi's is the most successful brand of jeans in the world and the business is still headquartered in San Francisco.

EXPLORE MORE!

Women and children also took part in the Gold Rush. You can read more about them in *Children of the Gold Rush* by Claire Rudolf Murphy and Jane G. Haigh and *The Gold Rush Kid* by Mary Waldorf.

AMERICAN CIVIL WAR

(1861–1865)

The American Civil War was fought between the Northern states and the Southern states. The Northern states had abolished slavery, or made it illegal, by the 1860s. But the Southern states wanted to keep slavery.

In 1860, Abraham Lincoln was elected the 16th US president. He was against slavery, but wanted to preserve the Union (keep the country together), not anger the South by ending slavery. Even so, people in the South did not want a president who was against slavery. The Southern states began to secede, or break away, from the rest of the country. They declared themselves a separate country, called the Confederate States of America. They even had their own president, Jefferson Davis. The secession of the Southern states started the Civil War. The Southern army, called the Confederate Army, was led by a general named Robert E. Lee. The Northern army, called the Union Army, was led by Ulysses S. Grant beginning in 1864. After the war, Grant served as US president for two terms.

On April 12, 1861, Confederate soldiers attacked the Union Army at Fort Sumter in South Carolina. These were the first shots fired in the war. The Union Army surrendered Fort Sumter the next day. Later that year, the Confederacy won the First Battle of Bull Run in Virginia. People were surprised because the Union Army had many more soldiers, so they were expected to win easily. The next major battle was the Battle of Shiloh on April 6, 1862. Both sides lost many soldiers. A total of 23,741 men died in only two days. On September 17, 1862, at the Battle of Antietam, the Union Army stopped Lee's advance, but that was the single deadliest day of the war.

On September 22, 1862, Lincoln introduced the Emancipation Proclamation. It was an order declaring all enslaved people should be set free. But two months later, when Lincoln gave his famous Gettysburg Address, the fighting still had not stopped. In his speech, he promised to keep fighting for enslaved people's freedom. The July 1863 Battle of Gettysburg turned the tide of the war as the Union stopped the South from coming north. Sadly, 51,000 soldiers died that day.

The end of the Civil War in 1865 meant that American slavery was abolished, and Northern and Southern states were no longer divided.

HISTORY REVEALED

In the 1870s, Jim Crow laws in the Southern states separated Black people from white people by segregating schools, pools, busses, bathrooms, restaurants, and drinking fountains into "Whites Only" and "Colored Only." These laws were still in place 100 years after slavery ended, until 1965.

EXPLORE MORE!

Read the historical fiction novel *Like a River* by Kathy Cannon Wiechman to follow the adventures of two teenage Union soldiers in the American Civil War.

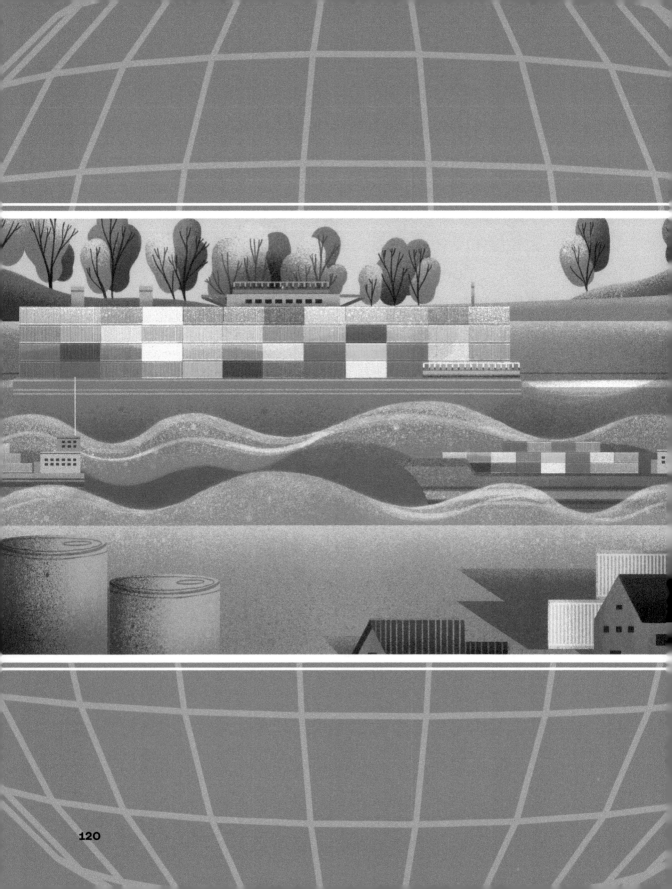

THE SUEZ CANAL AND THE SCRAMBLE FOR AFRICA

(1875)

The Suez Canal is a 120-mile (193 kilometers) artificial waterway that connects the Mediterranean Sea and the Indian Ocean via the Red Sea. Its construction connected continents and made moving cargo on ships much faster.

As global trade expanded, ships wanted a shortcut so that they would not have to go all the way around the continent of Africa. In 1869, the Suez Canal opened in Egypt. It allows ships to go directly from the Atlantic Ocean to the Indian Ocean through North Africa, via the Mediterranean and Red Sea. That cut the trip from London to the Arabian Sea by about 5,500 miles (8,850 kilometers).

Work on the Suez Canal began on April 25, 1859, and took just over 10 years to complete. Roughly 30,000 men were digging the canal at any given time. More than 1.5 million people, many of whom were unpaid and essentially enslaved, worked on the canal over the span of 10 years. Thousands died from diseases.

When the canal opened on November 17, 1869, it was under French control. Leaders from Egypt, Sudan, France, and America came to celebrate the new passageway. Opening the Suez Canal impacted world trade immediately. It let merchants circle the globe in a fraction of the time.

Egypt borrowed a lot of money from France and England to build the canal. When they couldn't pay it back, France and England took control of the country. This began what is called the Scramble for Africa, in which European countries raced to gain control of Africa, taking power by military force and influence. France, Spain, Germany, Italy, Portugal, Belgium, and England met to divide up African countries. Not one African leader was invited. During the Berlin Conference of 1884–1885, these European countries claimed they wanted to get rid of slavery, but they really wanted to control natural resources and convert African people to their religions, like Catholicism. One large diamond company, De Beers, took over the entire country of Rhodesia to mine diamonds. Africa went from being 10 percent under European control in 1870 to almost 90 percent in 1914. Only Ethiopia and Liberia stayed independent.

In 2021, a ship called the *Ever Given* got stuck sideways in the Suez Canal! The boat traffic backed up and caused a huge delay of deliveries to countries around the world. After almost a week, the *Ever Given* was freed and hundreds of ships continued on their way.

HISTORY REVEALED

Rubber, ivory, and diamonds were three main resources that Europeans stole from Africa. Blood diamonds, or conflict diamonds, are diamonds mined during times of war. The World Diamond Council estimates that more than 99 percent of diamonds are now mined legally.

EXPLORE MORE!

Would you like to learn how a canal works, with all its locks lowering and raising waterways? Read *Canals and Dams!* by Anita Yasuda, illustrated by Mike Crosier.

THE TECHNOLOGICAL REVOLUTION

(late 1800s–early 1900s)

The Technological Revolution, also called the Second Industrial Revolution, was a period when new inventions changed the way people lived. The introduction of the light bulb, the automobile, the telegraph, and the airplane made life easier in many ways.

Inventor Thomas Edison played a large role in the Technological Revolution. He ran what he called the Invention Factory in Menlo Park, New Jersey. He held more than 1,000 patents, or rights to technology that he invented. These included the record player, a movie camera, and, most famously, the light bulb, which he patented in 1879. Other inventors had created versions of light bulbs, but Edison's improvements made it possible for the light bulb to replace gas and oil lamps in homes and businesses. This meant that people could work later and factories could stay open into the night and make more products for people to buy.

The invention of the automobile was another huge advancement during this time. Many people are given credit for inventing the first automobile, but Germany's Karl Benz developed the first car in 1885. Then, in 1908, American Henry Ford made the Model T. He made assembly lines, where each person put a particular part on the car until it was completed. Automobiles allowed people to travel longer distances at higher speeds. This improved the economy. People were able to travel farther and faster to work, on vacation, or to restaurants, where they spent more money.

In 1901, Italian inventor Guglielmo Marconi sent the first transatlantic radio signal. His wireless telegraph took radio waves and transmitted Morse code, a series of signals (like beeps called dots and dashes) that let people communicate across long distances. His telegraph also made it possible to communicate to ships out at sea, which can help save lives after shipwrecks, including the 700 people saved when the *Titanic* sank in 1912!

On December 17, 1903, American brothers Orville and Wilbur Wright—who built some of the first bicycles—flew the first airplane, which they designed themselves. Even though Orville was up in the air for only 12 seconds and went just 120 feet, their success paved the way for the age of aviation. Travel across the country and around the world was now possible in a fraction of the time.

All these inventions and more made the Technological Revolution a pivotal time. It was a period of rapid advancement in communication, manufacturing, and transportation that changed the course of history.

HISTORY REVEALED

Another important discovery during this time was x-rays. Marie and Pierre Curie, husband and wife scientists, developed much of the technology needed for the x-ray machines that are used by doctors and medics. Some cancer treatments are also based on their work. Marie and Pierre Curie eventually earned a Nobel Prize for their work on radiation.

EXPLORE MORE!

Edison's work on the light bulb got a lot of help from an African American innovator named Lewis Latimer. Read about him in *Lewis Latimer: The Man Behind a Better Light Bulb* by Nancy Dickmann.

WORLD WAR I

(1914–1918)

World War I was the first global battle fought in many countries. It lasted four years and killed more than 20 million people. Europe was divided and other nations, like the United States and Russia, got involved.

In 1914, a Serbian man named Gavrilo Princip killed Franz Ferdinand, who was in line to be king of Austria-Hungary. European countries were already divided, and quickly sided with either Serbia or Austria-Hungary. Countries separated into the Central Powers of Austria-Hungary, Germany, Bulgaria, and the Ottoman Empire; and the Allies, also called the Entente Powers, which were Britain, France, and Russia. Italy, the United States, and other countries joined the Allies later. The war was fought on the Western Front from Belgium to Switzerland, and on the Eastern Front from the Black Sea to the Baltic Sea. Both sides also battled at sea to keep control of shipping routes.

New weapons were used in World War I. Airplanes flew overhead and tanks rolled through on the ground. German zeppelins, a kind of airship, spied on the enemy below and dropped bombs on Britain.

In 1917, the United States entered the war after the Germans sank a British ship, killing 1,197 people, 128 of whom were Americans. America also found out that Germany had asked the Mexican government to join Germany and fight against the United States. Mexico refused, but America went to war with Germany on April 6, 1917. The US Army placed posters of "Uncle Sam" to recruit more soldiers for the war. On November 11, 1918, it became clear that Germany and its allies could not win the war and a cease-fire was signed. Poppy flowers growing in the battlefields were worn to remember all the people who died. Of the 65 million men who fought in World War I, about 10 million died. Germany lost around 2 million soldiers, the most of any country. About 10 million civilians, or regular people who were not soldiers, also lost their lives. More than 20 million soldiers were wounded.

In the four years it lasted, World War I took many lives and destroyed Europe's economy. Europeans were left with very few working farms or factories. Then, in 1918, an influenza pandemic swept around the world and killed even more people than the war had. In 1918, the leaders of Germany and Austria stepped down, and, in 1919, Germany accepted responsibility for starting the war by signing the Treaty of Versailles. That finalized the end of the war.

HISTORY REVEALED

Germany may have signed the Treaty of Versailles, but its rising leader did not accept responsibility. Instead, he planned to attack the countries to which Germany owed money. A dangerous man named Adolf Hitler later started World War II and murdered millions of people, mostly Jews.

EXPLORE MORE!

Read the historical novel *Private Peaceful* by Michael Morpurgo for an exciting and heartfelt story about a boy fighting in World War I.

THE RISE OF COMMUNISM

(1911–1917 and beyond)

Communism is a form of government in which food, medical care, and resources are supposed to be spread around equally. But people's freedom is limited under Communism. Many world powers fought against Communist countries like Russia, China, and Cuba.

In 1917, Russian leader Vladimir Lenin started the first Communist government, which was led by the workers and peasants. It was based on Karl Marx and Friedrich Engels's pamphlet *The Communist Manifesto*. This form of government took over Russia, replacing the Romanov family, who had ruled for 300 years. Because they had a war going on inside their own country, Russia pulled out of World War I early.

From 1917 on, there was a civil war in Russia between the "red" Communists and the "white" forces, who opposed Communism. The Communist slogan was "Bread, Peace, and Land." After Vladimir Lenin died in 1924, Joseph Stalin took over. He killed anyone who ran away or spoke out against him. Stalin later made a five-year plan to build more farms and factories, but he did so with brutal force in his country over the span of 30 years.

For more than 2,000 years, China was ruled by an emperor. But in 1911, the people rose up and rebelled against the Qing dynasty. At the time, the emperor, Puyi, was only six years old! He had to give up his throne and China became a republic (a state in which power is held by the people and those they elect). This put an end to dynasties and imperial rule. For many years after the Chinese Revolution, there were battles over how China would be ruled and by whom. Lots of rebellion groups cropped up.

Eventually, the empire united as the People's Republic of China under Mao Zedong's rule in 1949. In 1958, Chairman Mao introduced a program called the Great Leap Forward. This created communes, or large communities, where more than 30,000 people worked and lived. Children were taken care of by other people so that mothers could work in the rice fields with their husbands. The program was a huge failure and led to a devastating famine, where people had no food to eat.

Cuba turned to Communism much later, in 1959, under Fidel Castro. The people of Cuba and China are not allowed free access to websites like Facebook, and the government tries to control how the news gets reported. From the 1940s through the 1980s, the United States fought the Cold War against Russia, China, and

Cuba. This did not involve shooting, but instead was a race to gather weapons and technology in order to prove who was more powerful.

HISTORY REVEALED

Many people in Communist countries today, such as China and Cuba, live in poverty. There have been revolts to overthrow Communist governments and, at times, the United States and other countries have placed embargos on, or stopped exporting goods to and importing goods from, Communist countries.

EXPLORE MORE!

Read *Political Science for Kids – Democracy, Communism & Socialism* by Baby Professor to learn more about Cuba, Russia, and other countries.

THE GREAT DEPRESSION

(1929–1939)

During the Great Depression, the global economy hit an all-time low. People were out of work, did not have enough food to eat, and struggled to survive.

World War I left many countries without enough money. The global economy slowed down in the late 1920s. The lack of jobs and food, the large debt that Britain, France, and the Allies owed the United States, and the reparations, or fines, that Germany owed the Allies made for very difficult times.

The United States was better off than Europe. American jobs had been created when the United States made planes and other supplies for the war. People started buying stocks, or shares of a company that could be sold to make more money. They also began using credit more often. But Europeans couldn't afford to buy or access what America produced and US banks fell apart. On October 29, 1929, the stock market crashed. Soon after, the unemployment rate (how many people are out of jobs) skyrocketed. These two factors brought on the Great Depression. People literally ran to the bank to get their money and were told that the bank didn't have it!

President Franklin D. Roosevelt made laws that protected people's money in the bank after that bank run. In 1933, shortly after he took office, he also created the New Deal. The New Deal formed several government agencies: the Federal Emergency Relief Administration (FERA) to help people without jobs; the Agricultural Adjustment Administration (AAA) to help farmers by raising the price of food; and the Public Works Administration (PWA), which built bridges, roads, post offices, and airports, putting lots of people to work.

In 1935, Roosevelt made the Second New Deal, replacing FERA with the Works Progress Administration (WPA), which created more than three million jobs. It also made the system of unemployment insurance, so that workers can get money if they are out of work. The banking system improved, and workers organized unions to improve conditions in factories and at schools. Still, millions of people were out of work, hungry, and homeless.

The Great Depression was felt around the world. Great Britain increased taxes on its people. In 1936, 200 shipbuilders marched 300 miles (about 480 kilometers) across England to beg the British government for help. In Germany, Adolf Hitler led the National Socialist German Workers' Party, also known as the Nazis. His rise to power led to World War II.

HISTORY REVEALED

During the Great Depression, life got so bad that people moved into shantytowns called Hoovervilles, named after President Herbert Hoover. The musical *Annie* has a song about these makeshift camps.

EXPLORE MORE!

Look for the award-winning historical novel *Bud, Not Buddy* by Christopher Paul Curtis to follow the story of a young boy on a quest to find his father during the Great Depression.

STALIN AND THE GREAT TERROR

(1936–1938)

Joseph Stalin was the leader of the Soviet Union, known today as Russia, until 1952. He led the Great Terror, in which millions of people were tortured and killed.

Joseph Stalin took over Russia (the largest country in the newly formed Soviet Union) and gave all his friends jobs. He did not take care of the Russian people and killed anyone who spoke out against him. Stalin led Russia in a way that made it an enemy of many countries, especially the United States. The United Socialist Soviet Republic, or USSR, was made up of 15 Soviet republics—Armenia, Azerbaijan, Belarus, Estonia, Georgia, Kazakhstan, Kyrgyzstan, Latvia, Lithuania, Moldova, Russia, Tajikistan, Turkmenistan, Ukraine, and Uzbekistan—and was in place from 1921 to 1991.

Joseph Stalin came into power after Vladimir Lenin died in 1924. Stalin was a Communist, which meant he wanted all products and systems to be owned and run by the whole community. Stalin had a five-year plan to convert Russia from a country filled with farms into an industrial stronghold. To reach this goal, Stalin instituted policies that killed eight million people, from professors to soldiers, and even regular citizens. Peasants had to work long, hard hours for very little pay. He promised the Russian people it was for the good of the country, but the people were still starving and cold.

The Great Terror, also called the Great Purge, was started in 1936 by Stalin and Nikolai Yezhov and lasted until 1938. In 1937, people were taken to prison, spied on, and accused of crimes that they had not committed. Stalin wanted to remove anyone who disagreed with him from the Communist Party and Red Army. An estimated 950,000 to 1.2 million people were murdered.

Former heads of the Communist Party were accused of trying to do away with the Soviet Union's government and bring back capitalism, an economy like the United States and Europe have now. They were taken to court in a series of three trials, called the Moscow Trials. The Moscow Trials were seen around the world. People could not believe that Lenin's friends and coworkers confessed to terrible crimes and begged to be put to death.

Poets, pianists, and theater directors were arrested, jailed, and often shot by a firing squad. During the Great Depression, many Americans had gone to Russia to look for work. These people were denied visas to travel back home. Many were also murdered. Due to Stalin's terrorist tactics, Russia and the United States were enemies for decades.

HISTORY REVEALED

Many people believe that the Moscow Trials were pure theater and that the people on trial were forced to confess. The trials were also known as "Stalin's Show." Some of the writers and artists on trial were saved, if Stalin liked their work.

EXPLORE MORE!

Read the historical novel *Breaking Stalin's Nose* by Eugene Yelchin for a story about a boy in the Soviet Union dealing with the arrest of his father, a high-ranking Communist.

SECOND SINO-JAPANESE WAR AND PEARL HARBOR

(1937–1945)

The Second Sino-Japanese War was fought between the Empire of Japan and the Republic of China. In China, it is also called the War of Resistance against Japanese Aggression. Pearl Harbor was when the Japanese attacked the United States, prompting the United States to enter World War II.

The Second Sino-Japanese War began on July 7, 1937, at the Marco Polo Bridge, when Japanese and Chinese troops fought in Peking (now called Beijing), the capital of China. This invasion of China by Japan started World War II in Asia. The Soviet Union and the United States helped China fight back against Japan.

It was the biggest war fought in Asia during the 20th century. Between 10 and 25 million Chinese people, and more than 4 million Japanese and Chinese soldiers, died or went missing.

The war happened because Japan wanted to increase its influence so it could get more resources, food, and workers. After World War I, the Chinese began making lots of textiles for clothing. That was not good for the Japanese economy. The Japanese, under Emperor Hirohito's command, invaded Manchuria in China.

As Japan kept taking over parts of China, the United States boycotted oil and steel exports to Japan in a show of support for China. Cutting off Japan's supply of oil and steel angered the Japanese.

So, on December 7, 1941, Japan attacked the US military base in Pearl Harbor, Hawaii. Even though there was a strong military presence in Pearl Harbor, Japan surprised the United States with 360 fighter planes and dive bombers. Entire ships were blown up and sank in minutes! In just over an hour and a half, more than 2,400 US soldiers and civilians were killed by bombs, torpedoes, and heavy shooting from Japanese pilots. The United States began to fight back.

The very next day, President Franklin D. Roosevelt declared war on Japan, and America entered World War II. The United States also gave more money to China. World War II ended when Japan surrendered on September 2, 1945. China got back all the land that Japan had stolen during the war.

The attack on Pearl Harbor is very important because that was what brought the United States into World War II.

At Pearl Harbor, there were 79 men who were sets of brothers and served together on the USS *Arizona*. Of those, 63 died in the Japanese attack and just one full set of brothers survived. Only four brothers were recovered and identified. The remaining 59 brothers are still unaccounted for. From then on, the US Navy did not let brothers serve together on the same ship because it was too much for a family to lose two, or three, sons at one time.

EXPLORE MORE!

Read *The History of Pearl Harbor* by Susan B. Katz for lots more information about the attack.

WORLD WAR II

(1939–1945)

World War II was a global conflict that involved many of the world's countries. It was fought because Adolf Hitler and the Nazi party in Germany were taking over countries by force and killing millions of Jewish people.

Nazi Germany's army invaded Poland in 1939. Britain and France declared war on Germany two days later. Yet this did not stop Adolf Hitler, the leader of Germany, from conquering France, Denmark, the Netherlands, Belgium, and Norway. Australia, Canada, New Zealand, the Soviet Union, and the United States joined the Allied Forces of Britain and France to stop Hitler from taking over Europe and the world. Germany formed the Axis powers with Italy and Japan.

The worst part of World War II was the Holocaust. At first, Jews were not allowed to own businesses, go to school, or have bank accounts. They were made to wear Jewish stars on their sleeves to identify them as Jewish. Then, late on November 9, 1938, Kristallnacht, or the "Night of Broken Glass," took place. German soldiers burned down synagogues (where Jewish people pray and worship), smashed the windows of people's homes, broke their china dishes and vases, and arrested 30,000 Jewish men. Those men were all taken away to concentration camps. Hitler and the Nazis rounded up millions more Jewish people, Romani, LGBTQ+ people, and disabled people. More than six million Jewish people and five million more from other groups died in concentration camps.

Jewish and non-Jewish people resisted what Hitler was doing and tried to go into hiding. Thousands of children were saved by efforts like the Kindertransport, a rescue effort that took Jewish children to other countries where they would be safe. One famous Jewish girl was named Anne Frank. She and her family were hidden in an attic in Amsterdam for years. Sadly, they were eventually betrayed and sent to a concentration camp, where she was killed.

On June 6, 1944 (D-Day), thousands of Allied troops landed in Normandy, France, to stop Hitler's plan. Finally, Germany surrendered on May 7, 1945. On May 8th, people danced in the streets to celebrate the end of the war. British and American soldiers liberated the people who were left in the concentration camps.

Even though Germany lost the war, the Japanese kept fighting until August 6, 1945, when the United States dropped an atomic bomb on the Japanese city of Hiroshima. More than 80,000 people, most of them civillians, were killed instantly. Then the United States dropped another nuclear weapon on Nagasaki, Japan, killing another 40,000 people. On August 15, 1945, Japan agreed to surrender. The surrender was signed on September 2, 1945, and the war was over.

HISTORY REVEALED

Albert Einstein and many other Jewish leaders created a Jewish nation-state called Israel in 1948 as a home for the Jews who were persecuted but survived the war. Because Palestinians, who are mostly Muslim, lived there as well, when the borders were redrawn in the Middle East, a conflict began that continues to this day.

EXPLORE MORE!

You can read *The Diary of a Young Girl* by Anne Frank or *Nicky & Vera* by Peter Sís to find out more about children during World War II.

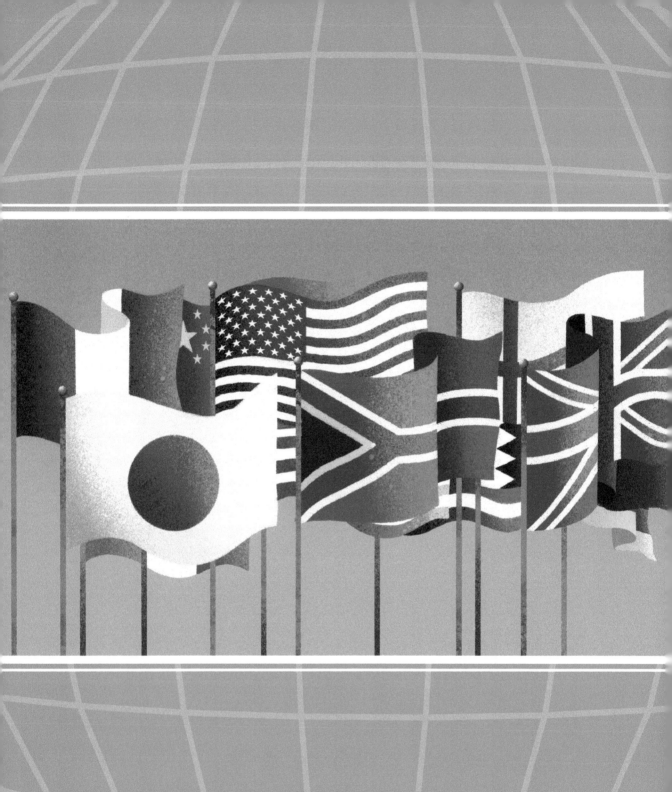

THE UNITED NATIONS

(1945–present)

After World War II, 50 countries formed the United Nations as an international organization that aims to maintain global peace and security, develop friendly relations among nations, and promote healthy living standards and human rights.

On October 24, 1945, the United Nations (UN) was formed. The UN is the most well-known and largest international organization with representation from countries all over the world. The headquarters are on international territory within New York City, and they have offices in Geneva, Switzerland; Nairobi, Kenya; Vienna, Austria; and The Hague, Netherlands. The original 50 countries included China, France, the Soviet Union, the United Kingdom, the United States, and many others. Now 193 member countries belong to the United Nations, which represents almost every nation in the world. Its logo has a globe surrounded by olive branches, which symbolize peace.

The UN began after World War II with the goal of preventing any future world wars. On April 25, 1945, leaders of 50 nations met in San Francisco, California, to discuss and draft the UN Charter, or the rules by which it would function. The charter was adopted on June 25, 1945, and took effect on October 24, 1945. The main purpose of the United Nations is to keep peace and security on a global scale and to protect human rights. This means giving food and medical supplies where there are local wars, famine, floods, fires, and other natural disasters. The UN also supports sustainable farming and environmentally responsible industries, and it upholds international laws.

Many countries in Africa, Asia, and Latin America got decolonized in the 1960s. Eighty former colonies joined the UN once they were independent from foreign rule. In 2012, the UN voted to allow Palestine to observe meetings without being able to vote.

In 2015, the UN Climate Change Conference took place in Paris, France. The United States and 194 other countries signed an agreement to cut down on greenhouse gas emissions. These countries are trying to prevent global warming from increasing.

The UN runs many agencies, like the World Bank Group, which loans developing countries money; the World Health Organization, which researches how to combat disease around the world; and the World Food Program, which delivers food to people who are hungry.

UNESCO is dedicated to education, sciences, and culture. UNICEF helps children worldwide.

HISTORY REVEALED

The original text of the Declaration by United Nations was written on December 29, 1941 by President Franklin D. Roosevelt, Prime Minister Winston Churchill, and Harry Hopkins, Roosevelt's assistant, with input from the Soviet Union. An earlier document, the Atlantic Charter, did not include religious freedom. Roosevelt insisted on adding it, and the Soviet leader Joseph Stalin eventually approved.

EXPLORE MORE!

For Every Child, a Better World by Kermit the Frog was written in cooperation with the United Nations and illustrates the UN's vision.

KOREAN WAR

(1950–1953)

Another country once controlled by Japan is Korea. Its leader, at the time, was Kim Il Sung. After World War II, Korea divided into two states: North Korea, which was Communist, and South Korea, which was democratic. Syngman Rhee became president of South Korea. When the North tried to take over the South in 1950, a war broke out that lasted for three years.

China and the Soviet Union supported North Korea because they were all Communist countries. The United States and the United Nations backed South Korea.

The United Nations sent in soldiers, led by US general Douglas MacArthur, to support South Korea. As the United States pushed invaders out of South Korea, North Korea's ally, China, swooped in to fight back. On June 27, 1950, US president Harry S. Truman commanded an attack by air and sea. Three days later, he sent in troops on the ground. Even though the US Congress has the power to declare war, according to the Constitution, it did not do that. Since World War II, Congress has never formally declared war.

As the struggle in Korea continued, the capital city of Seoul in South Korea was captured and recaptured four different times. The United States bombed North Korea for years. Fighter jets met in the air to combat, or fight, each other for the first time ever in history. Russia secretly flew overhead to defend Communist North Korea.

On July 27, 1953, the fighting stopped when the Korean Armistice Agreement was signed. It established a zone where there would be no military, called the DMZ (demilitarized zone), which now separates South and North Korea. It also let people who had been imprisoned in another country go back to their home country. Officially, the two countries are still at war because they never signed a peace treaty. In April 2018, North and South Korean leaders met to talk about moving toward peace.

The Korean War caused the loss of more than 815,000 soldiers' lives and millions of civilian deaths. Almost all of Korea's main cities were destroyed. More bombs were dropped on North Korea than were previously dropped on any other country in the world. Korea is still a concern for the world because if the North and South go to war, it could involve powerful and deadly nuclear weapons.

HISTORY REVEALED

The US Central Intelligence Agency (CIA) gathers information. During the Korean War, the CIA took Korean farm boys and turned them into spies. The 200 American agents the CIA hired did not speak any Korean. So it is now suspected that almost every agent made up his reports or was secretly collaborating with the Communists. They gave the United States a lot of false information.

EXPLORE MORE!

In the historical novel *Brother's Keeper* by Julie Lee, a young sister and brother must walk hundreds of miles to safety during the Korean War.

VIETNAM WAR

(1955–1975)

The Vietnam War was a battle between North Vietnam and South Vietnam. Both sides were supported by their allies. The United States was one of South Vietnam's allies. The war lasted almost 20 years and thousands of American soldiers and Vietnamese soldiers and civilians were killed.

The conflict involved Vietnam as well as Laos and Cambodia, which had been colonized by France. In 1954, a Vietnamese Communist leader named Ho Chi Minh led a revolt against the French and won. Vietnam was then divided into the North, which was Communist, and the South, which was not. But Communist rebels in South Vietnam, who were called the Viet Cong, wanted all of Vietnam to be Communist.

The United States did not want that to happen because they worried that would cause other Asian countries to become Communist as well. So they sent American troops to Vietnam to fight in the war. The Soviet Union, China, and other Communist countries supported North Vietnam. The United States, South Korea, Australia, Thailand, and the Philippines backed South Vietnam. They bombed North Vietnam in a military operation called Rolling Thunder and dropped a poisonous chemical called Agent Orange.

The war started on November 1, 1955, and ended with the fall of Saigon on April 30, 1975. The United States pulled out of the Vietnam War in 1973. By 1975, Vietnam, Laos, and Cambodia ended up becoming Communist.

The Vietnam War lasted for many years and between 966,000 and 3.8 million Vietnamese died during the war. Roughly 275,000 to 310,000 Cambodians, 20,000 to 62,000 people from Laos, and almost 60,000 US soldiers died or went missing in action (MIA). The Vietnamese Communist dictator murdered 2 million more of his own people.

Many Americans opposed the war. They did not think that the United States should be involved, especially after the United States killed many Vietnamese civilians. The United States also began bombing Cambodia in 1965. In the end, Communist troops took over Saigon in South Vietnam, renaming it Ho Chi Minh City. Vietnam united as a Communist country in 1976.

Many of the soldiers who fought in the Vietnam War and survived came home missing arms or legs. Some also have what is called post-traumatic stress disorder (PTSD). That makes it really hard for them to hear loud noises because it reminds them of the bombs and land mines exploding during the war. Thousands of Vietnam veterans have nightmares about their time fighting in the war.

It was a deadly and difficult war for the Vietnamese and the United States.

HISTORY REVEALED

Instead of dogs, the US Army used "people sniffers" placed in backpacks, or hanging from helicopters, to find enemies hiding in the jungle. The people sniffer was a device that detected human sweat. This mission was called Operation Snoopy, but the people sniffers often malfunctioned, alerting the American soldier to his own smell.

EXPLORE MORE!

You might want to read *Escape from Saigon: How a Vietnam War Orphan Became an American Boy* by Andrea Warren.

THE INDEPENDENCE OF INDIA AND PAKISTAN

(1947)

India was populated by many Muslim and Hindu people. After British rule ended, there was conflict over who would rule the land. Mohandas Gandhi, a Hindu leader and peacemaker, helped free India and Pakistan from Britain.

India was colonized by Britain and stayed under British rule for almost 100 years. The British charged Indians high taxes and did not treat them well. Gandhi started a movement to gain Indian independence in which he and his followers practiced *satyagraha*, or nonviolent resistance. Gandhi would go on hunger strikes, organize marches, and give speeches to rally people.

Gandhi led his followers on the Salt March in 1930. They spoke out against the taxes that the British government put on salt. They walked for 24 days and then broke the law by making their own salt from the sea.

Gandhi was put in prison many times. In 1942, Gandhi started the Quit India movement. He promised that India would support Great Britain in World War II if Great Britain agreed to leave India. On August 8, 1942, he gave a famous speech to thousands of people calling for nonviolent resistance. Instead, there was a lot of violence: Post offices, railroad stations, police stations, and other government buildings were burned, damaged, or destroyed. Eventually, India gained independence from Britain in 1947.

Still, tensions were rising between Muslims and Hindus. The two groups could not agree on what type of government they wanted and more violence erupted. The idea arose to split, or partition, India into two separate states. Almost all Indian Hindus would live in what is now India. Most Indian Muslims would live in West Pakistan (now the country of Pakistan) and East Pakistan (now the country of Bangladesh). It was very chaotic as millions of Muslims, Hindus, and Sikhs were forced to leave their homes. This mass migration was the largest in history.

Still, Indian people could not agree on which religion—Hinduism or Islam—would become the country's official one. Once again, Gandhi went on hunger strikes to stop the violence between Muslims and Hindus. Hinduism became India's official religion. Sadly, in 1948, Gandhi was shot and killed.

Gandhi's nonviolent ways influenced other leaders like Martin Luther King Jr. in the United States and Nelson Mandela in South Africa.

HISTORY REVEALED

Gandhi was not just a leader but was also a lawyer. He went to law school in London, and then moved to South Africa where he fought for the rights of Indian people. By the time he returned to India, his work was so well-known and admired that people called him "Mahatma," meaning "great-souled" or "holy one," as a title of respect. His birth name was Mohandas.

EXPLORE MORE!

You may want to learn more about Gandhi's work in *The Story of Gandhi* by Susan B. Katz.

THE COLD WAR

(1947–1991)

During the Cold War, Russia and the United States were at odds. They did not go to war with weapons, but they kept on guard and were enemies.

After World War II, the Soviet Union (Russia) and the United States were the world's most powerful nations. Both countries owned dangerous nuclear weapons that could destroy the world if they went to war. So, the communist Soviet Union and democratic United States began a "Cold War" that lasted more than 40 years.

While the two superpowers did not go to war with weapons, they did back opposing countries in other conflicts, spy on each other, and use scare tactics like flying planes into each other's airspace. The leaders during the beginning of the Cold War were Joseph Stalin in the Soviet Union and President Harry S. Truman in the United States.

Just before the Cold War started, Europe split into Western and Eastern Europe. Winston Churchill, the prime minister of the United Kingdom, called the invisible border in between these two regions the "Iron Curtain." In 1949, Germany was divided into two countries: East Germany (Communist) and

West Germany (democratic). The Berlin Wall was built between the two sides in 1961.

In the Korean and Vietnam Wars, Russia and the United States backed opposite sides. In Hungary (1956) and Czechoslovakia (1968), people rose up against Communism, but the Soviets crushed these uprisings and the United States decided not to intervene.

Cuba, an island just south of Miami, Florida, is also a Communist country. During the Bay of Pigs Invasion in 1961, Cuban exiles (people who had left the country), who wanted their leader Fidel Castro out of office, landed on Cuba's southwestern coast. The invasion was secretly paid for by the US government. Although it failed, the relations between Cuba, the United States, and the Soviet Union were damaged by this attempt. Then, in 1962, the Soviet Union placed nuclear weapons in Cuba, which upset the United States because the weapons were so close to US land. This led to the Cuban Missile Crisis, a 13-day standoff between the Soviet Union and the United States. This was the closest the two countries came to actual war.

The Cold War also involved an "arms race" where both the United States and Soviet Union manufactured lots of nuclear weapons, or arms. Luckily, none of those deadly weapons were ever used. In the late 1980s, US president George Bush and Mikhail Gorbachev, the leader of the Soviet Union, met to declare peace. The Soviet Union was weak and ended. The land was divided into many countries, one of which was Russia.

HISTORY REVEALED

During the Cold War, the Soviet Union set off nuclear devices to test them. Starting in the 1950s, kids in the United States did "duck-and-cover" drills in schools. President Truman ordered students to prepare in this way for a nuclear war. These are similar to what children do now for earthquake, tornado, or intruder drills.

EXPLORE MORE!

The Cold War Explained: A Pocket History for Kids by George Joshua gives you more information on this time period.

APARTHEID IN SOUTH AFRICA

(1948–1990s)

Apartheid was a system in South Africa that limited the rights of Black people, even though they were the majority. South African leader Nelson Mandela led the fight against apartheid and was put in prison for 27 years.

In 1948, the government of South Africa began making laws that took away Black people's right to vote, restricted where they could live and what jobs they could have, and made "whites-only" places like schools. This enforced racial separation was known as apartheid. The African National Congress (ANC) fought back in the 1950s and '60s, clashing with South Africa's National Party, which supported apartheid and was in power.

In South Africa, there was a hierarchy, like a ladder, of who had the most and least rights based on their skin color. According to apartheid, white citizens were at the top of society. Asians (including Indians) were next. After that came people of mixed race, and, finally, Black people were at the bottom.

The first apartheid law, passed in 1949, made it illegal for people to marry someone of a different race. Between 1960 and 1983, 3.5 million Black Africans were evicted from their homes and forced to move to one of ten designated "tribal homelands," or Bantustans. The government said that the people who had been removed and relocated would lose their South African citizenship.

Most of the white people in charge during apartheid were originally from France, Holland, and Germany. The United States and England opposed South Africa's treatment of people of color. The United Nations placed an embargo on South Africa, preventing the country from getting weapons or goods in order to pressure the government to end apartheid. By the 1970s and '80s, Black and Indian people in South Africa had started rising up against apartheid.

Between 1987 and 1993, the ANC and National Party negotiated to end segregation and let the majority rule. Apartheid was repealed, or undone, on June 17, 1991, and many ANC leaders were released from prison. Nelson Mandela, the leader of the ANC, had been arrested in 1962 and given a life sentence in 1964. He spent 27 years in prison. Amazingly, after Mandela was released, the country held its first democratic election in 1994 and Nelson Mandela won! He became the first president elected by the majority—both Black and white people.

Nelson Mandela worked alongside other activists such as Archbishop Desmond Tutu to end apartheid. However, South Africa's history of apartheid still impacts the country's society and economy today.

HISTORY REVEALED

Nelson Mandela earned his law degree in 1989, while he was still in prison. After that, he was granted hundreds of honorary degrees from universities around the world who admired his work against apartheid using nonviolent resistance. He died on December 5, 2013, when he was 95 years old.

EXPLORE MORE!

Talking Walls by Margy Burns Knight, illustrated by Anne Sibley O'Brien, is a wonderful book about all kinds of walls that have kept people apart, including Nelson Mandela's prison walls.

CIVIL RIGHTS MOVEMENT

(1954–1968)

During the civil rights movement, people organized, marched, and fought for Black people to have equal rights. Leaders like Martin Luther King Jr., Rosa Parks, John Lewis, and Malcolm X inspired masses of people to protest.

From the late 1800s all the way up until 1965, the United States had a system of segregation known as Jim Crow laws. Black Americans were separated from white Americans and had to attend different schools, swim in separate pools, and use different drinking fountains.

In the 1954 landmark case *Brown v. Board of Education*, the Supreme Court ruled that schools needed to be integrated and teach Black and white students in the same classrooms. Ruby Bridges was the first Black student to go to an all-white elementary school. She had to have police protection.

In 1955, Rosa Parks was arrested for refusing to give up her seat on a bus to a white passenger in Montgomery, Alabama. Martin Luther King Jr. led a yearlong bus boycott, where Black people refused to ride the bus. In 1956, the US Supreme Court decided that public transportation could no longer be segregated.

During the 1963 March on Washington, Martin Luther King Jr. delivered his famous "I Have a Dream" speech. As a result of King's leadership and the civil rights movement, the 1964 Civil Rights Act was passed. This act made it illegal to discriminate against people based on their skin color.

During the following year, 1965, Martin Luther King Jr. and his wife, Coretta Scott King, led a peaceful demonstration march from Selma to Montgomery, Alabama. It led to the Voting Rights Act of 1965. This act prohibited states from forcing Black Americans to take extra tests or pay poll taxes to vote.

Black Americans continue to advocate for fairness, equality, and respect. In 2013, a new movement called Black Lives Matter (BLM) started. Protests have broken out in every major city to celebrate Black lives and demand justice for the killings of unarmed Black people by the police.

The civil rights movement set the stage for other groups of people to fight for equal rights around the world. Protests, boycotts, and powerful speeches have sparked changes to laws and systems that affect the lives of Black, Latinx, Asian, LGBTQ+ people, and more.

HISTORY REVEALED

Civil rights leader Medgar Evers was the Mississippi field secretary for the National Association for the Advancement of Colored People (NAACP) and a US Army veteran. Even after *Brown v. Board of Education* desegregated schools, the University of Mississippi would not allow Evers to attend law school. Tragically, in 1963 he was assassinated by a member of the White Citizens' Council.

EXPLORE MORE!

Read *Black Leaders in the Civil Rights Movement: A Black History Book for Kids* by Glenda Armand to learn about 15 brave and inspiring people.

THE SPACE RACE

(1957–1975)

The space race was a time when the Soviet Union and the United States competed over which country could get to space first. Being in space was seen as a sign of power and technological advancement, so both countries literally aimed for the moon.

The Soviet Union launched the satellite Sputnik 1 in 1957. Then it sent Sputnik 2 with a dog named Laika aboard. Unfortunately, Laika did not return from her space mission.

The following year, in 1958, the United States launched its first satellite and created NASA (the National Aeronautics and Space Administration). The space race was another part of the Cold War, so schools started focusing more on math and science to prepare students for careers in engineering.

In April 1961, the Soviets sent Yuri Gagarin up into space. He was the first person to orbit the Earth. In 1965, Alexei Leonov, also of the Soviet Union, did the first "spacewalk" when he came out of the spaceship and floated around. There was even a stamp made with Leonov's spacewalk shown on it. The competition continued with the Apollo program in 1967 when the United States launched the Saturn V rocket.

Then US astronauts Neil Armstrong and Edwin "Buzz" Aldrin became the first men to walk on the moon on July 20, 1969. About 650 million people watched on TV as Neil Armstrong climbed down a ladder from the spaceship. He famously said, "That's one small step for [a] man. One giant leap for mankind."

Eventually, the Soviets and Americans decided to collaborate, or work together, and the space race ended in 1975. By 1984, the idea for an International Space Station (ISS) came about. The ISS is an artificial satellite where astronauts from many countries, including the United States, Russia, Japan, Italy, and Canada, do research. It takes the ISS about 93 minutes to circle the Earth, so it orbits our planet about 15.5 times a day.

So far, 242 astronauts, cosmonauts, and space tourists have gone to the ISS, from 19 different countries. Of that 242, there were 152 Americans, 49 Russians, 9 Japanese, 8 Canadians, and 5 Italians. A few people have gone back more than once. Space programs have also sent robots, called rovers, to Mars and other planets. Recently, a rover landed on Mars to collect soil samples and find out if there are any signs of life, like water. This international collaboration means that countries share information, which could help all humans in the future.

HISTORY REVEALED

Laika wasn't the first dog to go into space. On July 22, 1951, two dogs named Tsygan and Dezik were sent up by the Soviet Union, but not into orbit. These pups were the first living beings to come back from a spaceflight. Too bad they can't tell us what they saw!

EXPLORE MORE!

How about picturing yourself as an astronaut? *If You Were a Kid Docking at the International Space Station* by Josh Gregory, illustrated by Jason Raish, will help you lift off!

THE FALL OF THE BERLIN WALL

(1989)

The Berlin Wall was built in August of 1961 to separate the East and West German parts of the city of Berlin, and it was torn down in 1989. The fall of the wall meant that the two sides were reunified as one country, Germany.

The Berlin Wall was constructed around the East German–controlled part of Berlin in order to prevent East Germans from escaping to West Germany. It split apart families and left many, especially people in East Germany, feeling imprisoned in their own villages.

West Germans had a better life, with more money, stores, schools, and luxuries like candy and movie theaters. East Germans were poorer and controlled by a Communist government. Some East Germans tried to dig trenches to escape beneath the wall. Others built homemade hot air balloons to fly over it. Some hid in car trunks and tried to cross the border. Parents would hold up their children so their grandparents, who were trapped on the other side of the wall, could see them. At least 140 people died trying to flee East Germany. In June 1961, about 19,000 people snuck out of East Germany through Berlin. The next month, 30,000 left. On August 12, 1961, about 2,400 fled to West Germany—the most people ever to escape in one day.

On October 22, 1961, an American official was headed to the opera in East Berlin, but an East German border guard stopped him at one of the crossings, called Checkpoint Charlie. For 16 hours, American and Soviet tanks held a standoff at Checkpoint Charlie.

After the Soviet Union fell and Communism was banned, German people started to fight back against this type of government. The most concrete symbol of the Cold War was the wall dividing East and West Germany. On November 9, 1989, under pressure from protesters, the East German government announced that it would open the border with West Germany. People in both East and West Berlin began tearing down the wall.

That weekend, more than two million people went to West Germany to celebrate. Reporters said it was like a huge street party. Berlin had not been one unified city since 1945. Someone spray-painted "Is the war really over?" on a section of the wall.

East and West Germany did not officially reunify, or come back together, until October 3, 1990, almost a year later. The capital of

Germany was moved from Bonn back to Berlin, where it had been before the war. The fall of the wall opened borders, gave people freedom, and rebuilt lives.

HISTORY REVEALED

When the wall came down, people sat on top of or climbed it, and many people kept a piece of the wall as a reminder of its fall. They brought picks and hammers to break down the concrete. These people were called "wall woodpeckers." Bulldozers and cranes knocked down larger chunks. Many people still have their piece of the wall.

EXPLORE MORE!

The Wall: Growing Up Behind the Iron Curtain by Peter Sís is a great read about this time period.

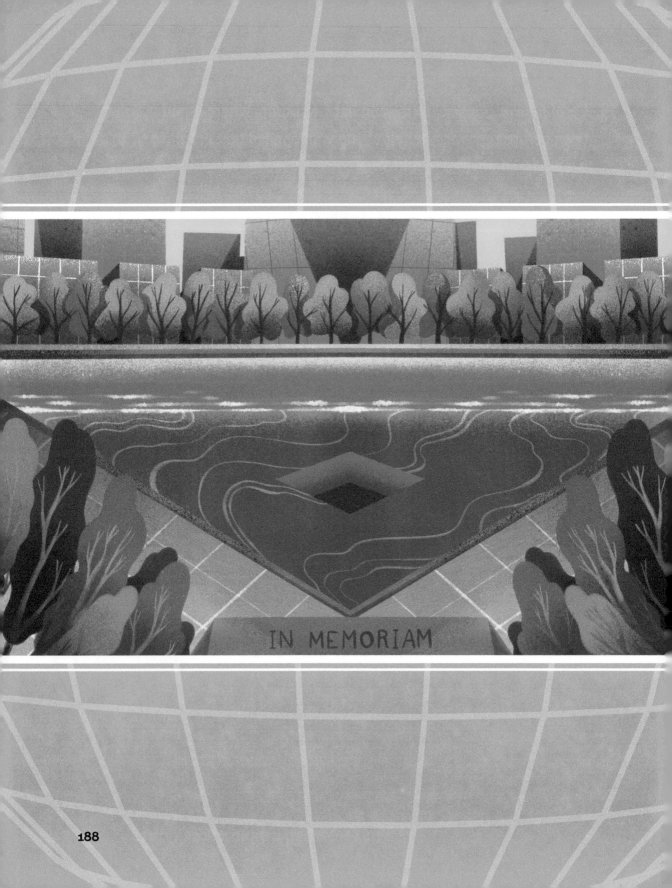

THE WAR ON TERROR

(2001–present)

The War on Terror involves the United States and other nations fighting to overthrow terrorist leaders like Osama bin Laden.

In 1990, the leader of Iraq, Saddam Hussein, ordered his troops to invade the country of Kuwait and take control of the oil reserves. The United States intervened to force the Iraqis out, leading to the Gulf War in the Middle East. From August 2, 1990, to February 28, 1991, 35 countries came together to fight back against Iraq's invasion of Kuwait. Operation Desert Shield was led by the United States from August 1990 to January 1991. Then combat really began through Operation Desert Storm. The United Kingdom and United States put troops in Saudi Arabia, and other countries joined in.

Then, on September 11, 2001, members of the radical terrorist group al-Qaeda hijacked, or took over, four airplanes. They flew two of them into the World Trade Center towers, killing thousands of people. The Twin Towers were the tallest office buildings in New York City. The planes hit the towers and exploded within 18 minutes of each other, and the massive buildings collapsed to the ground. The events on 9/11 were the worst attack on United States soil since Pearl Harbor. Almost 3,000 people died in the explosions and from the buildings collapsing.

A third plane crashed into the Pentagon, where many government officials work. All 64 people on board were killed, including the hijackers, as well as 125 people in the Pentagon. The fourth plane was also headed toward Washington, DC, but passengers found out what happened in New York and DC and overpowered the hijackers. Flight 93 crashed in a field in Pennsylvania.

The United States wanted to find the leaders of the terrorist group responsible for the 9/11 attack. So, it declared a war on terrorism and launched a series of attacks on Afghanistan, where al-Qaeda's leader, Osama bin Laden, was hiding.

In 2003, US president George W. Bush and British prime minister Tony Blair accused Hussein of having nuclear weapons and ties to al-Qaeda, the terrorist organization responsible for the 9/11 attack. Hussein was captured on December 13, 2003. Although no evidence of his direct link to al-Qaeda was found, he was hanged on December 30, 2006.

Nearly 10 years after the 9/11 attack, on May 2, 2011, US Navy SEALs led a raid, killing bin Laden, though the War on Terror is still ongoing.

HISTORY REVEALED

A memorial was built where the Twin Towers once stood, and New York constructed a new tall building nearby. This new tower, One World Trade Center, opened on November 3, 2014. The names of the nearly 3,000 people killed by the terrorist attacks on September 11, 2001, are etched in a marble wall surrounding a reflection pool.

EXPLORE MORE!

Towers Falling by Jewell Parker Rhodes is a good book to read to learn more about 9/11.

MODERN TECHNOLOGY

(1970s–present)

Over the past 50 years, there have been many technological changes and advances. Personal computers, cell phones, and social media have transformed the way we communicate with each other. Websites and apps like Facebook, Twitter, Instagram, Snapchat, TikTok, and Amazon allow people to share information and buy products quicker than ever before.

In the beginning, the internet was more of an *intra*net. For example, college students could communicate with other students at their university, but not with people outside the school. In the 1970s, personal computers became available, and in 1989, the World Wide Web was invented. Now people could use their computer to access information from all over the world, and get it fast! They no longer had to look things up in large reference books called encyclopedias or go to a library. With the internet and email, people could now stay connected to friends and family much more easily.

Cell phones were introduced in 1973. Since then, they have changed from being just a device to make calls to being a minicomputer that fits in our pocket. Texting allows us to send a message to someone in another room—or another country. And the message is received almost immediately. You can also ask and get answers to questions just by talking into your phone.

In 2004, Facebook was launched. Since then, people have used Facebook and other social media platforms to organize political protests and even revolutions! When rallies, protests, or other events happen, people can decide when and where to meet by using social media through their phones.

Technological advances have also made it easier for people to communicate their needs by posting messages online. A person waiting for an organ donor can post a message and get connected to a person on the other side of the world who is the right match. When disasters happen, like floods and earthquakes, people can post what supplies they need, and others can donate those items. Long-lost friends or family members can use the internet to find each other and be reunited.

Changes in technology have changed our world. Today, you can chat with someone on video using tools like Zoom or FaceTime. You can watch a movie on your smartphone or write a novel on your tablet. Through advances in technology, people can now find information, stay connected, and solve problems easier and faster than ever before.

HISTORY REVEALED

The ancestors of cell phones were called car phones and were actually installed into a car but looked just like a phone that you would have in your house. They were not perfect and used a technology different from that of modern cell phones. Anyone with a radio could listen in on your conversation.

EXPLORE MORE!

Read *How the Internet Changed History* by Carol Hand or *The Story of Inventions* by Catherine Barr and Steve Williams, illustrated by Amy Husband.

PARIS AGREEMENT ON CLIMATE CHANGE

(2015–present)

The Paris Agreement, also known as the Paris Climate Accord, is an international treaty aimed at stopping climate change. It was adopted by 195 countries and the European Union (EU) in Paris on December 12, 2015, and first enforced on November 4, 2016.

The goal of the Paris Agreement is to decrease global warming to between 1.5 and 2 degrees Celsius. In order to reach this milestone, countries around the world are supposed to limit their emission of greenhouse gases, pollution made when factories and cars emit chemicals. The idea is to create a climate that is not warming in temperature by 2050.

This is a landmark agreement because it is the first time that nations from around the world agreed to try and fight climate change. Climate change leads to the warming of the oceans, which causes more hurricanes, tsunamis, droughts, wildfires, and floods.

The treaty works on five-year plans. In 2020, countries submitted their plans to take action on climate change. These are known as nationally determined contributions (NDCs), in which countries outline how they will cut down on their greenhouse gas emissions. These NDC plans also report specific actions countries will take to adapt to the rising temperatures around the globe.

The Paris Agreement also includes a framework for countries to support each other with money, technology, and training. By 2024, countries will report about how and what they are doing to combat climate change and adapt to already rising temperatures. They will also report what support they have given or need. For example, manufacturing more electric or hybrid cars cuts down on carbon emissions.

The Paris Agreement has already created many low-carbon solutions and "green," or environmentally friendly, markets. Lots of cities, states, and countries are making carbon neutrality targets. These are zones where they hope not to produce any carbon emissions. Using wind or solar power instead of coal helps reduce carbon emissions. Electric, solar-powered, or hybrid cars also create new business opportunities and jobs.

There is nothing on this planet that we all share as humans more than the air, water, and land. The Paris Agreement is a crucial effort to stop, or slow, global warming.

HISTORY REVEALED

Take a deep breath! Did you know that forests produce roughly 20 percent of the Earth's oxygen through photosynthesis? Most of the oxygen we breathe (more than 50 percent) is made by plants in the ocean called phytoplankton. So if the rain forests get cut down, and the oceans warm up so much that marine plants can't survive, we will have a real problem!

EXPLORE MORE!

Greta Thunberg, a young environmentalist and activist from Sweden, wrote *No One Is Too Small to Make a Difference.*

THE COVID-19 PANDEMIC

(2019–present)

At the end of 2019, a new strain of coronavirus spread around the world. Millions of people got sick and died. SARS-CoV-2 (COVID-19) led to the closing of stores, schools, restaurants, theaters, and other gathering places around the world.

Scientists and doctors believe that the coronavirus (COVID-19) spread from an animal, possibly a bat or a pangolin, sold in a market in Wuhan, China. Viruses can spread from animals to people and be very deadly. Visitors to and from China who became infected carried the virus to other countries. COVID-19 quickly spread across the globe.

Hospitals were overwhelmed with patients who were very sick and could not breathe. On March 11, 2020, the World Health Organization declared COVID-19 a global pandemic, or worldwide disease. Life changed dramatically for people all over the world. Schools closed and students moved to online learning. Grocery stores were allowed to remain open, but people had to wear masks to go inside because the virus was spread in the air. Churches, mosques, temples, and synagogues had to shut their doors because it was feared that large gatherings of people would cause a "super-spreader" event. Many countries closed their borders, refusing to let international travelers enter. People were told to stay home as much as possible, avoid spending time with people outside their household, wash their hands often, and try not to touch their eyes or nose. Everyone was asked to maintain a "social distance" of six feet from other people to reduce the risk of infection.

Amazingly, researchers were able to create a vaccine in less than a year. Administration of the vaccine began in December 2020. There is still no cure for COVID-19, but with the vaccine, many people are now protected from getting very sick and dying.

The coronavirus pandemic changed how our whole world functioned. People spent much more time at home. Families could not visit one another, particularly older people like grandparents who were especially at risk. Birthday parties, weddings, funerals, and other important events were canceled or held online.

As of September 2021, more than 219 million people have gotten COVID-19 and 4.55 million people have died from it worldwide. The pandemic is not over at this time, with new and more contagious variants still emerging. However, the availability of vaccines has provided hope that getting the pandemic under control is possible.

HISTORY REVEALED

Many people who get COVID-19 lose their sense of smell and/or taste. Researchers still do not know for sure why this happens, but it occurs in roughly 18 to 41 percent of patients who have COVID-19.

EXPLORE MORE!

A Kids Book about COVID-19 by Malia Jones helps explain this virus in more detail.

Acknowledgments

I appreciate: my editor, Mary; my publicist, Ariel; my parents, Janice and Ray; my brother, Steve; my writers' group—Andrew, Brandi, Chris, Evan, Kyle, and Sonia; my nephews Sam, Jacob, and David, and my nieces, Sofia and Katherine; my supportive family and friends: Susan, Ann and Greg, Jeanne, Deborah, Kiernan, Laurie, Tanya, Carla, Julia and Ira, Maureen, Amparo, Michael, Ricardo, Alejandra, Arden, Jen, Tami, Karen, Annie, Jessica, Marji, Lara, Anita & Bob, Jerry, Nena and Mel, Jami, Stacy and Rick, Michelle R., Violeta, Diana y Juanca, and Sylvia. in memory of my Grandma Grace, Aunt Judy, Ilse and Bill. Special thanks to Darryl Robinson, Crystal Spearman, Chalmers Knight, Michelle Geller, Jim Chrystal, and Michael Harron for being incredible sensitivity readers. —SBK

About the Author

 **Susan B. Katz**, NBCT, is an award-winning, bestselling, bilingual author, National Board Certified Teacher, educational consultant, and keynote speaker. She taught for more than 25 years. Susan has 20 published books with Scholastic, Penguin Random House, Simon & Schuster, Callisto/Rockridge, Capstone, and Heinemann. *The Story of Ruth Bader Ginsburg* hit #18 on Amazon's overall bestseller list and #9 among all kids' books. Ms. Katz served as the Strategic Partner Manager for Authors at Facebook. When she's not writing, Susan enjoys traveling, salsa dancing, and spending time at the beach. You can find out more about her books and school visits at SusanKatzBooks.com.